CW01010956

ONCE UPON A RHYME

IMAGINATION FOR A NEW GENERATION

Cambridgeshire

Edited by Donna Samworth

 Young**Writers**

First published in Great Britain in 2004 by:
Young Writers
Remus House
Coltsfoot Drive
Peterborough
PE2 9JX
Telephone: 01733 890066
Website: www.youngwriters.co.uk

SB ISBN 1 84460 443 8

Foreword

Young Writers was established in 1991 and has been passionately devoted to the promotion of reading and writing in children and young adults ever since. The quest continues today. Young Writers remains as committed to engendering the fostering of burgeoning poetic and literary talent as ever.

This year's Young Writers competition has proven as vibrant and dynamic as ever and we are delighted to present a showcase of the best poetry from across the UK. Each poem has been carefully selected from a wealth of *Once Upon A Rhyme* entries before ultimately being published in this, our twelfth primary school poetry series.

Once again, we have been supremely impressed by the overall high quality of the entries we have received. The imagination, energy and creativity which has gone into each young writer's entry made choosing the best poems a challenging and often difficult but ultimately hugely rewarding task - the general high standard of the work submitted amply vindicating this opportunity to bring their poetry to a larger appreciative audience.

We sincerely hope you are pleased with our final selection and that you will enjoy *Once Upon A Rhyme Cambridgeshire* for many years to come.

Contents

Hannah Lamonte (10)   49
Rebekah Lawrence (10)   49
Fatima Shah (10)   50
Matthew Davis (10)   50
Rebecca Adamson (10)   51

Coates Community Primary School
Lucy Skerritt (11)   52
Robin Hutchinson (11)   53

Fulbridge Junior School
Kasim Shariq (11)   53
Fashiha Ashiq (9)   54
Kiran Rashid (9)   54
Ceri Pollard (9)   55
Shannon Zajac (8)   56
Daniel Baillie (9)   57
Emma Henchman (8)   57
Rumaanah Raqeeb (8)   58
Heena Saleem (10)   59
Jessica Trower (11)   59
Daniel Wright (10)   60
Saba Zia (9)   60
Henna Sajjad (9)   61
Hina Iqbal (10)   61
Matthew Gentleman (9)   62
Asad Hussain (10)   62
Waqas Hussain (8)   63
Hassan Ahmed (8)   64
Kiran Kaur Sohi (11)   65
Shelby Summers (11)   65
Sehrish Ahmed (9)   66
Rukhsaar Ali (11)   67

Gunthorpe Primary School
Keipher Ormesher (10)   67
Daniel Twinn-Waters (11)   68
Ryan Launchbury (9)   69
Ashley Newstead (10)   70
Charlie Kingston (9)   70

Sophie Knight (9)	71
Ainsley Robertson (10)	71
Callum Bowyer (9)	72
Stacey Cann (10)	72
Natasha Stones (9)	72
Daniel Smith (9)	73
Chloe Frisby (10)	73
Olivia Gourlay (10)	73
Samantha Burns (9)	74
Jake Moore (9)	74
Jake Church (9)	74
Nathan Setchfield (9)	75
Nicole Duffy (9)	75
Hannah Cooper (9)	75

John Clare Primary School

Hettie Davies (10)	76
Evangeline Rata (9)	76
Tara Lepore (7)	76
Ethan Brooks (10)	77
Angharad Davies (9)	77
Olivia Fricker (9)	78
Jessica Bradley (10)	78
George Wilson (11)	79
Amelia Markham (11)	79
Leo Rytina (10)	79
Scott Roberts (8)	80
Jessica Shaw (8)	80
Kelly Stockwell (8)	81
Lewis Jackson (9)	82
Emily Seaton (9)	83
Molly Webster (8)	83
Hugh Markham (9)	83
Hannah Morton (9)	84
Jason Grandidge (8)	84
Hayley White (9)	85
Jemima Davies (7)	85
Lindsey Irons (9)	86
Leo Davies (7)	86
Harriet Warren (11)	87

Leighton Primary School

Keanu Parkinson (10)	87
Chelsea Budden (9)	88
Samantha Longman	88
Bethany Hawes (10)	89
Xeña Howlett (11)	89
Declan Higgins (10)	90
Norton Crowson (11)	90
Jonathan Kingston (9)	91
Rosie Horton-Williams (10)	91
Andrew O'Sullivan (10)	92
Aaron Lowey (9)	92
Georgina Amey (10)	93
Christopher Greenacre (11)	93
Christle Boyden (10)	94
Ben Syder (10)	94
Clare McGrath (10)	95
Georgia Paul (11)	95
Molly Edgar (10)	96
Farah Anverkhan (11)	96
Alexandra Doyle (9)	97
Victoria Cartledge (9)	97
Jemma Harber (10)	98
Shannon Doyle (9)	98
Louise Hooper (10)	99
Alice Chapman (10)	99
Clare Foster (11)	100
Jemma Horton (11)	100
Paul Barnes (11)	101
Tamara Hole (10)	101
Danielle Patterson (10)	102
Dylan Wilson (9)	102
Samantha Cartledge (10)	103
Michaela Peacock (10)	103
Rebecca Meech (10)	103
Nikki Fletcher (11)	104
Connor Gray (10)	104
Cameron Feguson (10)	104
Alarnah Smith (9)	105
Luke Brace (9)	105

Meridian Primary School

Annie Veenman (10)	106
Hannah Chandler (11)	106
Natasha Leigh-Wootton (11)	107
Frankie Surmon-Böhr (10)	107
Charlotte Hallworth (11)	108
Jacob Morris (11)	108
Phoebe Sharratt (11)	109
Holly Sheppard (10)	109
Annie Gregory (10)	109
Charlotte Horne (11)	110
Helen Spence-Jones (10)	110
Stephanie Cousins (11)	110
Zoe Bishop (9)	111
Alex Sinclair (11)	111
Alyssa Smith (9)	112
Abbie Peek (8)	112
Daisy Frame (10)	112
Elizabeth Turland (8)	113
Hannah Albone (10)	113
Sarah Mallinson (11)	113
Emily Jameson (9)	114
Aliénor Longson (9)	114
Chloë Bidwell (9)	115
Liam Sutton (9)	115

Middlefield Community Primary School

Linda Campo (10)	116
Gregory Mason (10)	117
Jacob Dawson (10)	118
Mark Dawson (9)	119
Harrison Smith (10)	120
Lorna Childs (11)	121
Rebecca Willard (10)	122
Lincoln Miles (10)	123
Douglas Shillito (11)	124
James Poulton (10)	125
Jethro Steel (11)	126
Samantha Mitchell (11)	127
Luke Thomas (10)	128
Abagail Rothwell (10)	129

Thomas Warne (11)   130
Samuel Page (9)   130
Jonathan Fromant (9)   130
Daniel Birkinshaw (11)   131
Jamie McDonald (10)   131
Ryan Gore (10)   132
Cory Houghton (9)   132
Aiden Clarke (11)   133
Ryan Pearce (11)   133
Brady Mayes (10)   134
Jordan Reynolds (9)   134
Benjamin Miles (10)   135
Hannah Cooley (10)   135
Liam Hill (10)   136

Parnwell Primary School
Oscar O'Brien (10)   136
Sophia Lane (11)   137
Katie Evans (11)   137
Scott Neil (10)   138
Katie Andresen (11)   138
Aidan Bates (10)   139
Peter Denton (11)   140
Emma Smith (11)   140
Jasmine Joyce (11)   141
Joel Gomes (10)   141

Priory Junior School
Christopher Bates   142
Jamie Butler (10)   143
Jessica Miller (9)   143
Faith Hewitt (10)   144
Daniel Biddle (9)   145
Jade Ursell & Josh Woodend (9)   145
Adam Williams (10)   146
Liam Brook (9)   146
Nicole Searle (10)   147
Thomas Bryon (9) & Alastair Guinee (10)   147
Heather Linnell (10)   148
Jack Bramley (9)   148
Jordan Adams (9)   149

Robyn Staddon (9)	177
Alyssa Ruston (9)	178
Philip Mitchell (10)	179
Nathan Donnachie (9)	180
Jacob Hoster (9)	181
Alice Dimmock (10)	182
Jennifer Polhill (9)	183
Grace Richards (10)	184
Lewis Miller (10)	185
Scott Griffiths (9)	186
Charlie Hoxley (9)	187
Matthew Nicholson (9)	188
Andrew Laverty (10)	189
Stuart Entwistle (10)	190
Seana Banks (9)	191
Rachael Bailey (9)	192
Jack Leenderts (10)	193
Emma Christie (10)	194
Jade Hewitt (9)	195

Queen Edith Community Primary School

Amy Hastings (9)	195
Cordelia Chui (8)	196
Anna Collins (9)	197
Ajit Niranjan (10)	197
Laura Di Paolo (11)	198
Charlotte Bowden-Pickstock (10)	199
Karim Ahmed (10)	200

West Walton Community Primary School

Jack Woodcock (10)	200
Ben Perrett (10)	201
Lee Plume (11)	201
Ben Gilding (10)	202
Elliott Quinn (10)	202
Daniel Cowling (11)	203
Edward Stagg (11)	203
Kay Duggan (11)	204
Jac Goult (11)	204
Emily Bouch (10)	205
Jake Masham (11)	205

Sarah Gathercole (10)	206
Liam Gowler (11)	206
Robyn Vickers (10)	207
Eilish Quinn (10)	207
Karl Parry (11)	207
James Woolford (11)	208
Hannah Gathercole (10)	208
Danielle Kirk (10)	209
Ashley Racey (11)	209
Abigail Barnes (11)	210
Lauren McLeod (10)	210

Wilburton VPC School

Eliot Lees (10) & Jade Glennon (9)	211
Haydn Jones & Lewis Povey (10)	212
Toby Hill (9)	213
Nedeane Robinson (9)	214
Crystal Seppings (9)	215
Amy Few & Ella Myhill (10)	216
Thomas Harris (11) & Luke Massey (9)	217

The Poems

Left Out

Tears fall from my face
My loneliness grows and spreads
I have no friends
I hear them playing
I feel the sadness, the bitter taste
The world is not a good place to be
Me.

Rebecca Smith (10)
Abbots Ripton CE Primary School

Happiness

A white blanket of snow
People crunching through the snow
Someone throws a snowball and it hits my mouth
A lovely hot drink.

Jenna Bates (9)
Abbots Ripton CE Primary School

The Happiness Of A Newborn Sister

My newborn sister, soft and tiny and perfect
My newborn sister, smells of baby lotion
My newborn sister, smiles just for me
My newborn sister, speaks my name just for me
My newborn sister, hungry for life.

Kerry Higgins (10)
Abbots Ripton CE Primary School

Unfairness

I feel angry with them
I can smell the jealousy in the air
'Go to your room!'
'But I didn't do it!'
I can taste fire and ice
They are playing but I am not allowed
Just because
I'm the youngest.

Charlie Upshall (10)
Abbots Ripton CE Primary School

Excitement Is . . .

I smell the air changing
I feel impatient for the freshness of tomorrow
My heart is beating rapidly
I dream pictures of my adventure in my mind
Yes, I'm going to Disneyland
I can taste the holiday ice cream already.

Keri Cooper (10)
Abbots Ripton CE Primary School

Lost

Fear rushing towards me
No way out of this dreadful prison
My body tenses
My head is filled with noise
Help!

Lewis Bacon (10)
Abbots Ripton CE Primary School

Trauma

He smells the fear in the cage around him
Slowly strangling him.
He tastes the fear, why him?
He sees the phone, Childline?
They'd get him.
He hears the door open.
They're coming, they're coming, they're coming.
He feels hard blows from an abusive hand.
He runs
But
Where can he hide?

He is traumatised.

Allegra Scales (10)
Abbots Ripton CE Primary School

I'm Hungry

L ovely, soft, squidgy sponge,
U nique smell of frying chips,
N ow it's time for the sizzly eggs,
C reamy chocolate custard,
H ot and tasty food,
    hunger.

Amelia Sykes (9)
Abbots Ripton CE Primary School

They Don't Care . . . It's So Unfair!

They touch you, say sorry
But, they don't care.
You smell it, cookies baking, they won't share
But, they don't care.
You hear them playing music on their CD player,
I don't have one,
But, they don't care.
A horrible, dry taste in my mouth won't go away,
But, they don't care.
I see her getting what she wants,
I don't,
But, they don't care.

Or do they?

Jack Huckle (9)
Abbots Ripton CE Primary School

Loneliness

Loneliness is not a good sight, standing all alone
Loneliness smells like old times
You can't touch loneliness but you can feel it inside.
Loneliness tastes like being alone
Nobody should be lonely
Nobody should be alone.

Carolyn Daly (9)
Abbots Ripton CE Primary School

Anger!

Electric needles
Burning inside
Sour thoughts
Hot bubbling lava
Volcano erupting
I'm ready to explode.

Victoria Custerson (10)
Abbots Ripton CE Primary School

Jealousy

When you can touch happiness,
But you can't actually have it.

When you can smell other people's happiness,
But you can only smell your own fear.

When you see other people playing with their dogs,
But your one has gone.

When you can see other people playing in the park,
But you can only hear your mind saying, 'Ha, ha!'

When your friends can taste the wealth of the world,
But all you can taste is *Hell!*

Brogan Pett (10)
Abbots Ripton CE Primary School

Without Him

An empty space inside
Sadness
Grey faces
Salty tears on my cheek
Weeping

I'll see him again
Someday.

Emma Brown (10)
Abbots Ripton CE Primary School

Happiness On Christmas Day

The crackling of the cosy fire
The awaiting presents wanting to be opened
The smell of the fine fir tree
The roast potatoes cooking
The gleaming snow covering the ground
In a thick blanket.

William Lygo (11)
Abbots Ripton CE Primary School

Anticlimax

The day after the awe-inspiring snowstorm,
It turns to slush.
The excitement that ran through my veins,
Escapes into the atmosphere.
The trees are stripped of their jewels,
They stand bare,
The day after the awe-inspiring snowstorm,
I stand and stare.

Kate Keohane (10)
Abbots Ripton CE Primary School

Rejection

I hear nothing, nobody wants me.
Everything is spinning.
I taste the rejection in my mouth.
It's in the air so plain and bare.
Rejection I can touch, so sharp it hurts.
I hear nothing, nobody wants me.

Scarlet-Holly Broker (11)
Abbots Ripton CE Primary School

Loneliness

People push me like I don't exist
I can smell my own fear
I hear them playing without me
A single salty tear runs into my mouth
People stare at me, smirking
But I know . . .
I'm not alone.

Amber Manfroi-Lynn (10)
Abbots Ripton CE Primary School

Waking Up

I open my eyes and the light stabs them,
I feel them burning.
Suddenly aware of my room,
I feel it suffocating me.
The stickiness of my mouth
Deprived of fresh air.
With my ear to the pillow, sweating,
I hear the humming, tingling sounds of my body.
I sense the blurriness of the world,
The never-ending world.
I am confused for that short second
Until I sort out my world and
Wake up.

Lewis Clarke (10)
Abbots Ripton CE Primary School

Happiness Is . . .

Happy, excited people
The taste of success when you have a birthday
The lovely dinner
When you get a fizz in your tummy.

Ryan Drage (10)
Abbots Ripton CE Primary School

Thunder And Lightning

It sparkles like my girlfriend's eyes
It is like a wolf that howls at night
It is a powerful spike
That hits you at night.

Ryan Atkinson (11)
Alderman Jacobs School

Night

She screams like a werewolf,
She has glowing, blue eyes,
She is black and gently roaring,
The glittering stars make coordinates,
They are shimmering and sparkling
Like yellow eyeballs,
She is like shining moonlight,
She is gleaming,
She is as sweet as a butterfly,
The stars can be
Her eyes.

Elizabeth Butcher (10)
Alderman Jacobs School

Snow

A white blanket covers the ground
It suffocates the grass
Snowflake ballerinas dance in the sky
Snowman stares at you
From the garden
His watchful eye follows you.

Luke Ilsley (10)
Alderman Jacobs School

Wind

The wind fiercely blows windows open and shut,
She screams noises, opening cupboards,
She sweeps the leaves off the trees,
She swoops down,
Scattering stones everywhere.

Deanna Spendelow (11)
Alderman Jacobs School

Hail

As hail falls around
He is an icy wind running down
Small bombs clutter the streets
He is hurting innocent souls with his hard thrust
Tapping on windows
Hurtling on doors
Attacking the ground in minutes
He gives no mercy
He has rage and anger
He is like a bee stinging you with all his might
He breaks umbrellas
He has no fear
At the end, hail waits once more.

Sian Mulqueen (10)
Alderman Jacobs School

Frost

The shine from frost
Will sparkle in your eyes,
Although the sparkle
Will come to life.
The touch of frost
Will melt wherever,
But if the weather will ever change.
As the frost flows
Side to side in the sky,
The frost will land before you
As it lands on you.

Lewis Moat (10)
Alderman Jacobs School

Thunder

Thunder growls like a wolf
He tries to scare you
He sounds like a volcanic volcano
Erupting in the sky
He moans and groans with indigestion
Thunder fades away
Like sugar in a cup.

Hayden Ruggles (11)
Alderman Jacobs School

The Sun

The sun is sparkly like a gold ring,
His eyes are red,
He speaks like a dragon in the night,
His nose smells like a fire in the night,
His cheeks are glittery like the stars,
Finally the night goes to bed,
Until the next morning.

Chanel Webb (11)
Alderman Jacobs School

Night

Night has eyes that are always watching you
Then he shouts to try and scare you
The night is a bear scratching on the windows
The night is wet like a thunderous storm.

Jonathan Hastings (10)
Alderman Jacobs School

The Rain

The rain has dripping tears,
Filled with loneliness.
He is gently falling to the ground,
The cloud is crying,
He is spitting water onto the floor.
He is a snail slithering down a wall,
Swaying to and fro.
The rain is eyes
That are watching you . . .
Everywhere!

Chelsie Smith (11)
Alderman Jacobs School

Night

Night has golden, gleaming eyes
That shine upon you.
Stars shimmer and stare above you.
The moon is fearsome like a big bad guy.
You can hear animals,
Growling until morning comes.
The gruesome moon gradually disappears.

Natalie Guild (10)
Alderman Jacobs School

Night

Night is like a gloomy forest
With waving trees surrounding the air.
The moon is like a face looking down on you,
She knows it frightens you.

Holly Istead (10)
Alderman Jacobs School

The Sun

The sun is like a phoenix
She will destroy anything that approaches
She makes huge explosions of power
She makes fire waves that can kill a man from 500 miles
She destroys comets and meteorites from miles away
Nothing can survive her scorching hot heat.
She never goes to sleep.

Rory McCourt (10)
Alderman Jacobs School

Night

The night falls into a deadly sight
Eyes gleam at me there and everywhere.
Smashing windows fall down on my arm.
A puff of perfume stinging my eyes.
God is watching us from up above
And beyond the nightfall.

Stacy Quince (11)
Alderman Jacobs School

Day

The day sparkles as it glitters in the sky
He looks with his shiny, glowing eye
He eats the silver clouds in the sky
His blue, shiny eyes look at us when we are sad
Come out and play with the sky.

Julie Rogers (11)
Alderman Jacobs School

Thunder And Lightning

Thunder is an erupting volcano
Lightning is like a flashing torch.
His brother, Thunder, is his best friend.
When they meet they make terrifying noises,
Like a car crash in the night.
It ends with a power cut.
Then Thunder goes back home.

James Brundell (10)
Alderman Jacobs School

Lightning

Lightning is like daggers in the sky
He is like electricity hitting the ground
He makes me feel lonely when sparks fly in the sky
He dances on the smoother surfaces
It is like a flashing light crashing down on the ground.

Chloe Hilliam (10)
Alderman Jacobs School

Night

The night is like a black spider,
In a witch's home.
The sky is like a piece of coal
That burns in a fire.

Jessica Jardine (10)
Alderman Jacobs School

The Night

The night floats by with dark red eyes,
Snaking between buildings,
With the moon shining,
Powerful, like a laser.

Thomas McCulloch (10)
Alderman Jacobs School

A Candle

A candle with a glimmering flame,
Illuminates the room.

A candle flickers,
Like a lost child,
Burning brightly,
Against the darkness.

A glimmering light,
Fights the night,
Burning the wax so bright.

A fragile light,
Is in the night,
Flickering bright,
Then sleeping so tight.

William Griffin (10)
All Saints' CE Junior School

Flame

F ire burning bright,
L ulling you to sleep,
A ngry fierceness flickering
M alignantly in the dark,
E yes glittering in the haze.

Dominic Nolan (10)
All Saints' CE Junior School

Candle Flame

I have a red flame
I am not tame
I dance on my wick
I shimmer and flick
I blaze in the dark
I can light up and jerk
I can move, I can lurk
I shine, am divine
I'll keep you hot
I am a lot like a flame
I am good but can cause pain
I can kill and I can grill
I can keep you alive
But I still often surprise
I'm not to touch
I don't burn much
I am glowing, I am flowing
I can sparkle, light up dark still
I cast shadows on your faces
I am elegant, the greatest
I'm a . . . candle.

Rachel Wright (11)
All Saints' CE Junior School

Flame

F lames glowing in the darkness
L ight flickering and dancing
A n amazing sight twinkling
M elting away into a puddle of smooth wax
E ventually gone, that beautiful shine.

Luke Reid (10)
All Saints' CE Junior School

Bonfire Night

There is nothing in the dark sky,
Then suddenly there's a spray of silver,
A raging outburst of red,
People jumping up and down in excitement.
A colourful sky has been created.
Bang, bash, crash, flash!
People running about amazed,
They're trying to see all the fireworks.
Catherine wheels emerge,
Then shimmer away.
Rockets fly up in the sky, explode!
Sparklers light up the night.
There's colour in the sky,
That twinkles in your eye.
The fireworks disappear,
The dark sky returns,
People walk away.

Liam Hänisch (8)
All Saints' CE Junior School

Candle

C alm and relaxing,
A ngry flames dancing,
N ew orange and blue flames light up,
D elicate sparkles,
L azy and sleepy,
E legant shadows.

Cairo Felix (10)
All Saints' CE Junior School

Bonfire Night

A really still, still, dark sky
It has little light that the stars made
Suddenly there were sparkly colours
There were noises like
Zoom, bang, boom, sparkle, whiz!
The fireworks already started
The sky has created a shower of sparkly colours
A silk of silver
A glowing of gold
A pinch of purple
An explosion of yellow
A rainbow of red
A sparkle of blue.

Stephanie Leung (8)
All Saints' CE Junior School

Bonfire Night

An empty sky waiting for light,
Suddenly *pop, squeal, bang!*
Rockets burst, bubbling purple.
A pool of blue colour in the sky.
Catherine wheels fall to the floor.
Children jumping up and down.
Nerves, children squealing and shouting.
Then broken candles, rockets,
Squeals, bangs and crackles,
Just lay as mice.

Charlotte Hudson (7)
All Saints' CE Junior School

Bonfire Night

Crowds of people waiting
For the fireworks to start,
When suddenly,
Whizz, bang, crash and *twinkle!*
Rockets zooming,
Roman candles shimmering
And Catherine wheels twirling.
What a beautiful sight.
All the beautiful colours,
Like a rainbow at night.
Bonfire burning,
Red, orange and yellow.
What a wonderful night we have had,
All the colours die down.

Irena Radić (7)
All Saints' CE Junior School

Bonfire Night

A crowd of people are waiting for the fireworks to start.
Suddenly, *bang, pop, whizz, crackle!*
A spray of silver!
A burst of blue!
A pop of purple!
A ray of red!
An outburst of orange!
Catherine wheels come out at night,
People say, 'What a wonderful sight!'
Rockets go up into the air,
People shout and wave and stare.
When the moon is shining bright,
People say, 'What a fantastic night!'

Olivia Still (8)
All Saints' CE Junior School

Bonfire Night

A black, calm, boring old night,
Suddenly a spray of colour appears!
We all cry out for more, more!
Bang, pop, sparkle, whiz!
Fireworks explode all around us.
A fountain of colour,
Lights the night sky.
Whizz went the Catherine wheel,
Sparkle went the sparklers,
Rockets spray silver,
Bonfire crackling hot and warm,
Roaring flames dance up high,
All fireworks have gone
And the black, calm, boring old night returns.

Rebecca Brown (8)
All Saints' CE Junior School

Happiness

Happiness is going to the cinema,
Happiness is playing with my shadow,
Happiness is being in my mum's arms,
Happiness is friendship,
Happiness is going to the fair,
Happiness is fun,
Happiness is great!

Callum Hay (7)
All Saints' CE Junior School

If I Were . . .

If I were a giant
I'd stamp around all day
And want to eat children
In a greedy sort of way.

If I were a teacher
I'd make children have detention all day
And let the school be fun
In a strict sort of way.

If I were a ghost
I'd come out all day
And scare children out of their skins
In a see-through sort of way.

Isobel MacDonald (7)
All Saints' CE Junior School

Bonfire Night

The sky is pitch-black,
We all wonder what's going to happen next,
Then suddenly a loud screeching noise.
Young ones stay in the parents' arms anxiously,
Dogs bark from the streets,
The sky illuminates with bright colours,
Children jump with delight.
Then it finishes off with seven multicoloured Catherine wheels,
Spinning fast at the same time.
The show ends,
Children's faces turn into a frown,
Sadly they walk home.

Matthew Brigham (8)
All Saints' CE Junior School

Bonfire Night

The night was still and dull.
Or was it?
A little light was appearing.
It got bigger and bigger.
Suddenly the whole sky lit up with colour.
Catherine wheels spinning.
Rockets racing.
A ray of red.
A splash of silver.
A garden of gold.
An outburst of orange.
A rainbow of brightness.

Scarlett Blades (8)
All Saints' CE Junior School

A Recipe For Happiness

A pinch of love
And a swirl of friends
A pretty dove
From the heavens above
Add a cupful of laughter
And a bowl of smiles
A handful of stars
Which can go on for miles
A bar of chocolate
And a ride from the fair
All these things you have to bake
To make a fun-filled, happy cake.

Sean Wilson (11)
All Saints' CE Junior School

Happiness

Happiness is my mum loving me,
Happiness is flying my kite,
Happiness is being in my mum's arms,
Happiness is playing in my playhouse,
Happiness is my friend playing with me,
Happiness is my school,
Happiness is my teacher,
Happiness is in my heart,
Happiness is going on my bike,
Happiness is my grandmother,
Happiness is eating sweets,
Happiness is peace,
Happiness should be in everybody's heart,
Happiness is love around the world.

Florence Bradshaw (7)
All Saints' CE Junior School

Bonfire Night

The sky is full of colour
A garden of green appears
Bang, boom, crackle, twinkle!
Little people go inside for safety
A burst of blue appears
Sparklers twirl all around
People stare in amazement
Fire gets hotter
A Catherine wheel makes a twirl
What a colourful night
Everyone jumps up.

Zanib Raja (7)
All Saints' CE Junior School

What Am I?

I am the dancer wearing yellow and blue,
Dancing on my stage of wax,
But still I have no arms and legs.

I am the one who soothes,
With a glow,
Yet I have no candle.

I am the one who is man-made,
With a swish of a match
I am born,
But yet my life is short.
What am I?

Answer: candle flame.

Verity Gibson (10)
All Saints' CE Junior School

Bonfire Night

A black, dull, boring sky,
Suddenly a ray of light,
All different colours
Bang, crash, pop, sizzle, whizz
And then gasps,
The most amazing firework!
A vibration of violet,
After a while the flames start leaping,
Eventually they die down
And the sky is dull and boring again.

Amy Lister (7)
All Saints' CE Junior School

What Would I Ask Of The Wizard Of Oz

If only I could be more organized,
I would definitely be able to revise,
For those deadly horrible SATs,
I especially hate the maths!

I would be playing outside happily,
Instead of doing my homework angrily,
Or I could be chatting away on the phone,
Licking ice cream on a cone.

I would fly to China and back (if only I had a plane),
Or become a movie star having lots of fame,
But instead I sit bored to death in my old home,
Organising my things all on my own!

Zahra Ahmed (10)
All Saints' CE Junior School

Bonfire Night

A blank sky, no one can see anything
And then *bang!*
More and more and more.
Bang, bang, bang, bang!
Everybody gets excited.
The biggest outburst of orange,
A garden of green,
A gizzle of gold.
I noticed flames leaping from the fire,
Then all I can see are the stars.

Edward Adamson (8)
All Saints' CE Junior School

The Candle

This warming, calming manner,
Is produced on a dark night,
In the house, the power has gone,
The candle evaporates the fright!

The darkened eyes of the people,
Glitter as the candle burns,
The red, the blue, of the flame,
The wax to liquid it turns!

Elegantly, the flame dances,
A light breeze comes from the door,
As the dance is about to stop,
It prances around once more!

The small, white candle,
It becomes less and less,
Keep away from children,
For the top they may press!

Abigail Reynolds (10)
All Saints' CE Junior School

Happiness

Happiness is me skateboarding
Happiness is loving a family and a family loving you
Happiness is peace
Happiness is my mum coming out of hospital
Happiness is all the food and drink we have
Happiness is the lovely gardens to play in
Happiness is the lovely insects that flutter in the gardens
Happiness is joy around people.

Joe Hancock (7)
All Saints' CE Junior School

The Candle

You can trust a candle,
When electricity is gone,
When there is a power cut,
The candle flame burns on.

Its flame will dance and flicker,
Like it's having fun,
But it can look cross or violent,
The candle flame burns on.

It smells of smoke and burning wick,
The odour is so strong,
Its light makes moving shadows,
The candle flame burns on.

There are lots of candles,
And of flames, there's more than one,
But they always look so beautiful,
The candle flame burns on.

The flame may dwindle and then die,
Then the light is gone,
But if you light it up again,
The candle flame burns on.

Susan Burberry (11)
All Saints' CE Junior School

Candle Poem Acrostic

C andle glowing in the dark,
A n angry, violent, blueish spark,
N ot much light, very dim,
D ancing calmly above the rim,
L ike a raindrop tall and thin,
E xhausted the flame goes out,
     leaving a thin wax skin.

Lucy Evans (10)
All Saints' CE Junior School

Bonfire Night

In the garden, all is peaceful,
When suddenly, *zoom, crash, bang* in the sky!
A burst of blue,
A garden of green is waiting for you.
A ray or red and white fireworks, like it's snowing.
A big, exploding firework like the rainbow.
Watch them for a while.
A bonfire blazes.
Catherine wheels whizz, sparklers shimmer.
Then everything stops . . .
The night sky returns back to normal.

Charlotte Wilson (8)
All Saints' CE Junior School

Bonfire Night

The night sky is black
Suddenly a shower of stars,
A burst of sparkle
And shining colours,
A pop of purple, a ray of red
Catherine wheels swirl and twirl,
The fireworks die down,
The sparklers started
They whirl and twirl in the night sky.

Rebecca Hammond (7)
All Saints' CE Junior School

War

War is dark red
It smells like smoke and fumes
It tastes like a poisonous drink
It sounds like guns firing and people dying
War lives in the heart of a devil.

Anna Steward (10)
All Saints' CE Junior School

Candle Poem

Beautiful flame,
Glowing and casting shadows.
The wick is burning,
Glazing reflection.
The wick is melting away,
Glowing reflection.
Glittering flame,
The wick is smooth and shiny,
A burning, thin wick.

Christopher Brown (11)
All Saints' CE Junior School

Candles

C alm, a colourful flame,
A ngrily, the candle rages,
N arrowing, the flame becomes thin,
D azzling, the hypnotizing candle,
L uminous, you can see it from miles around,
E legant, the yellow and blue flame,
S parkly, a glittering sight.

Jack South (10)
All Saints' CE Junior School

Flame

F urious, burning fire,
L ulling watchers to sleep,
A ngry, raging flame,
M ean, hot, burning, creating
E legant shadows.

Kasim Khan (10)
All Saints' CE Junior School

Candle Poem

Dancing in the dark,
Suddenly I jump away,
From the candle wax.

Melting from the heat,
Shriveling slowly away,
Trying to escape.

Stuck into the wax,
Mounted the flame is on me,
Standing all alone.

Ryan Hughes (10)
All Saints' CE Junior School

Disease

Disease is black
It smells like onion
Disease tastes like a mouldy, black, mushy banana
It sounds like a fire alarm ringing in your ears
It feels cold and rough
Disease lives in dirty, pitch-black, deserted houses.

Evie Johns (9)
All Saints' CE Junior School

Happiness

Happiness is baby pink,
It smells like lavender.
Happiness tastes like sugar,
It sounds like birds tweeting.
It feels like silk,
Happiness lives in our heart.

Taylor Brady (9)
All Saints' CE Junior School

What Would I Ask Of The Wizard Of Oz?

If I could meet the Wizard of Oz
I'd ask him for more determination because
I may already have some of it
But only a little bit.

If I have tried my very best
I must forget about the rest
And try not to let it worry me
It's too late to change it now, you see!

To have more self-confidence
May make a difference
And really just to believe that I
Cannot give it more than my very best try!

Charlotte Burroughs (10)
All Saints' CE Junior School

What Am I?

If any draught catches me
I sway from side to side,
I can be different colours
All at the same time.

I stand up tall
Like a soldier,
Ready to obey orders.

I am mysterious and beautiful,
Sometimes I may flicker.
Do not be afraid of me,
All I may do is glitter.

Emily Gaylor (11)
All Saints' CE Junior School

Candle Flame

C rackling flame,
A mazing glow,
N ight-time warmth,
D ripping wax,
L ighting up the room,
E legant flame, swaying in the dark.

F lame floating on the wick,
L iquid substance surrounds the flame,
A dmired by everyone,
M elting wax,
E yes glittering around the flame.

Alix Gunn (10)
All Saints' CE Junior School

Candles

They're the head of an arrow,
Sitting there in sorrow,
When the lights go dead,
They guide you to bed,
But when there's a slight breeze,
They dance like swaying trees,
Dots from left to right,
Going high and low at a different height,
They can be spooky and calm,
So you can use them wherever you are.

Tom Syer (10)
All Saints' CE Junior School

Happiness

Happiness is pink,
It smells like flowers in a breeze.
Happiness tastes like something sweet,
It sounds like laughter.
It feels soft and bouncy,
Happiness lives in your heart.

Amber Larkinson (9)
All Saints' CE Junior School

Happiness

Happiness is baby pink,
It smells like luscious flowers whispering in the breeze.
It tastes like strawberries and cream.
Happiness sounds like sweet music,
It feels soft and smooth.
Happiness lives in the centre of sweet-smelling roses.

Sophie Nugent (9)
All Saints' CE Junior School

Happiness

Happiness is sunshine-yellow.
It smells like flowers whispering in the breeze.
It tastes like sweet toffee ice cream.
It sounds like everlasting laughter.
It feels fluffy and soft.
Happiness lives in the sunshine of our smiles.

Hannah Reid (9)
All Saints' CE Junior School

War

War is pitch-black.
It smells like toxic gas.
It tastes like engine oil.
It sounds like someone alive, screaming,
                              whilst being burnt.
It feels like being bitten by a rattlesnake.
It lives in the souls of devils.

John Tenerowicz (9)
All Saints' CE Junior School

Truth Is Blue

Truth is blue.
It smells like lavender.
Truth tastes like minty chewing gum.
It sounds like the breeze through leaves.
It feels like silk.
Truth lives in a distant universe.

Janna King (9)
All Saints' CE Junior School

Frustration

Frustration is deep blue,
It smells like smoke floating in the breeze.
Frustration tastes strong and spicy,
It sounds like someone clicking fingers constantly.
It feels sticky and crumbly,
Frustration lives in a deep, hot, cursed forest.

Eve Parsons (10)
All Saints' CE Junior School

Hate

Hate is blood-red
It smells like burning rubber
It tastes like Brussels sprouts
It sounds like someone screaming
It feels rough and bumpy
It lives in the centre of the Earth.

Gregory Evans (9)
All Saints' CE Junior School

Love!

Love is baby pink
It smells like melting milk chocolate
Love tastes like a fresh strawberry smoothie
It sounds like a beating of your heart
It feels as soft as a fluffy cushion
Love lives in your heart.

Charlotte Holmes (9)
All Saints' CE Junior School

Happiness

Happiness is pink
It smells like perfume
Happiness tastes like a fresh packet of strawberries
Happiness sounds like people giggling
It feels like silk rubbing against your face
Happiness lives in you and me.

Sophie Walton (9)
All Saints' CE Junior School

Anger

Anger is the colour of red, black and grey.
It smells of choking black smoke.
Anger tastes of grit with a touch of fire.
It sounds like chanting voices of war.
Anger feels like pain and suffering.
It lives in everything and everyone.

Emma Baruah (9)
All Saints' CE Junior School

War

War is dark red,
It smells like hot fire burning,
War tastes burnt and bitter,
It sounds like the Twin Towers crashing together,
It feels rough and strong,
War lives in the heart of evil.

Zara Tariq (10)
All Saints' CE Junior School

Boredom

Boredom is grey
It smells like burnt toast
Boredom tastes like Rich Tea biscuits
It sounds like grown-up talk
It feels like a flat football
Boredom lives in school.

Benjamin Wright (9)
All Saints' CE Junior School

Peace

Peace is white
It smells like the gentle smell of lavender
Peace tastes like strawberry yoghurt
It sounds like calm waves lapping on top of each other
It feels smooth and silky
Peace lives in your heart.

Sophie Still (9)
All Saints' CE Junior School

Hope

Hope is a white shimmer,
It smells like lavender mixed with the morning's dew,
Hope tastes like ice cream on a hot day,
It sounds like the flutter of birds taking flight,
It feels as soft as a horse's winter coat,
Hope lives in the world, somewhere.

Jessica Wing (10)
All Saints' CE Junior School

Wealth

Wealth is gold
It smells like perfume
It sounds like coins clattering
It feels like chocolate running through your finger
Wealth lives in a palace.

Awais Ali (9)
All Saints' CE Junior School

Death

Death is a blood-red colour.
It smells like diseased, rotten flesh.
Death tastes like cheese which is stale and mouldy.
It sounds like people screaming in pain.
Death feels like a white-hot iron dropped on your hand.
Death lives in *Hell.*

James Hawes (9)
All Saints' CE Junior School

War

War is blood-red.
It smells like smoke at its worst.
War tastes like burnt toast.
It sounds like drums drumming.
It feels rough and sharp like sandpaper.
War lives in the hearts of evil people.

Hafsah Sarfraz (10)
All Saints' CE Junior School

Joy

Joy has all the vivid colours of a rainbow
It smells like freshly baked garlic bread
Joy tastes like barbecue flavoured crisps
It sounds like the laughter of children
It feels like bouncing on a bouncy castle
Joy lives in cloud nine.

Callum Shea (9)
All Saints' CE Junior School

War!

War is *red*
It smells like smoke drifting through the air
War tastes like vinegar mixed with eggs
(And someone insane)
It sounds like the scream of a soldier dying for his country
It feels like the pain of a bullet in your heart
It lives in trenches waiting to kill civilization again.

Charlie Hancock (10)
All Saints' CE Junior School

Hatred

Hatred is raging black!
It smells like burning rubber.
Hatred tastes crunchy and sour.
It sounds like gunshots being fired in a war.
It feels like spiky and jagged rocks.
Hatred lives in the horrible, mean side of your heart.

Nathan Stephenson (10)
All Saints' CE Junior School

Happiness

Happiness is rainbow-coloured
It smells like a freshly cooked curry
It tastes like candyfloss
Happiness sounds like laughter
It feels soft
It lives in our hearts.

Holly-Ann Warman (10)
All Saints' CE Junior School

Candle

I am a wick burning,
Gently and slowly the light moves,
I look up at the light,
The light sparkles at me,
It twinkles and the wax begins to melt,
The wax melts and it becomes a big puddle,
Once it is gone I can smell smoke and I turn black.

Isma Bi (10)
All Saints' CE Junior School

A Candle

C almly flickering in the dark
A beautiful glowing light
N o wind blows the flame
D ancing gracefully in its own light
L ight of dawn has come
E xtinguished, for no longer needed.

Tara Fitzpatrick (11)
All Saints' CE Junior School

Death

Death is jet-black,
Death smells like a burning mattress,
Death tastes like brandy,
Death sounds like thunder,
Death feels sharp, pointy and ragged,
Death lives in Hell.

James Murphy (10)
All Saints' CE Junior School

A Candle

A bright beam
Glistening from a candle light
Oh, so bright
Flickering
From a small candle flame
Swaying from side to side.

A bright gleam of burning light
Guiding me through the dark night.

Wax has drifted
Drifted slyly off the surface
Slithering slowly around
Like a snake
Searching for its prey.

A bright gleam of burning light
Guiding me through the dark night.

Thomas Iuliano (10)
All Saints' CE Junior School

What Am I?

I am the thing that melts the wax,
That's really bright
And makes people relax.
With my flickering flame
I can be violent,
And I can be noisy
And I can be silent.
What am I?

Answer: a candle.

Andrew Williams (11)
All Saints' CE Junior School

What Would I Ask The Wizard Of Oz?

Tolerance, tolerance, tolerance!
All I need is tolerance,
To go and listen to people's views,
They can do exactly what they choose,
I will do just as they say,
Not do it the other way,
Or they could do the same for me,
But I won't ask for it forcefully,
Just as long as we both get exactly as we wish,
Maybe in a silver dish!
Tolerance, tolerance, tolerance!
All I need is tolerance,
To listen to another's quote,
To give them my full vote,
To tell them exactly what I think,
Not to give them another wink.
Tolerance, tolerance, tolerance!
All I want is tolerance!

Isabella Tocco (10)
All Saints' CE Junior School

A Candle

A frail flame flickers,
Dancing to the wind's song,
Interfering with the expanse of darkness.

The room is dimly lit,
Indigo, amber and gold,
Casting soft shadows on the walls.

Dwindling, dwindling,
The flame dies down,
The last glimmer of hope.

Gone.

Lola Hale (10)
All Saints' CE Junior School

What Would I Ask Of The Wizard Of Oz?

If I could ask the wizard,
For what I wanted to,
I would ask for patience,
Well, wouldn't you?
I'd watch some people get it wrong,
Then help them try again,
Especially if they're younger than me
And I have long been ten.

I would put up with other people,
Asking what they should do.
I would keep my temper
And my friends too!
I'd be able to play patience,
The game Solitaire,
I would keep my patience gracefully
And not just pull my hair.
If I had some patience,
I would not shout or bark
And on my reputation,
I would not leave a mark!

Sam Gascoigne (10)
All Saints' CE Junior School

A Candle

A candle illuminates the dark room,
A candle casts shadows on the wall,
A candle sways when a draught comes in,
A candle glowing on the dark table,
A candle fiery and yellow,
A candle burns the white, squashy wax,
A candle gives out a little beam of light.

Daniel Perkins (11)
All Saints' CE Junior School

What Am I?

My first is in cat,
But not in rat.
My second is in mad,
But not in mud.
My third is in nut,
But not in put.
My fourth is in dog,
But not in hog.
My fifth is in light,
But not in kite.
My sixth is in power,
But not in flour.
My seventh and eighth are in flounder,
But not in rounder.
My ninth is in Ami
And also in cattle.
My tenth is in melt,
But not in belt.
My eleventh is in reign,
But not in rain.
What am I?

Answer: candle flame.

Amy Setchfield (10)
All Saints' CE Junior School

A Candle

Flicker, flicker
Candlelight
Burn for me during the night

Flicker, flicker
Candlelight
Oh, you are so bright

Flicker, flicker
Candlelight
Your flame is thin and elegant

Flicker, flicker
Candlelight
With a pointed flame like a raindrop

Flicker, flicker
Candlelight
Always casting shadows that give me a fright.

Zahra Mansha (11)
All Saints' CE Junior School

A Candle

Oh, flickering flame,
You are ever so bright,
You give this room,
A touch of light.

Oh, candle, candle,
With a touch of flame,
If you burn the wax,
It's not your fault.

Oh dear, dear candle,
Just keep on glistening,
Just sit there brightly
And keep on listening.

Umber Nawaz (10)
All Saints' CE Junior School

A Candle

Stay with me, candle,
Don't blow out,
You're my friend in the dark.
Gleam little candle,
Gleam and glow.

Stay with me, candle,
Don't blow out,
Keep me warm in the cold night.
Dance little candle,
Gleam and glow.

Stay with me, candle,
Don't blow out,
Stay by my side until morning.
Glimmer little candle,
Gleam and glow.

Isabella Gamble (10)
All Saints' CE Junior School

A Candle

In the dark, cloudless night,
All I see is a glowing light.
It flickers about,
Like a wild hound
And as it moves,
It makes a crackly sound.

In the dark, silent house,
There's only a candle,
As small as a mouse.
All around it there's a golden glow,
Moving gently,
To and fro.

Pietro Di Meglio (10)
All Saints' CE Junior School

A Candle

Candle, candle
Burning bright
I do so hope you last the night

Candle, candle
Burning bright
I see you through the winter's night

Candle, candle
Burning bright
Save me from the monsters of the night

Candle, candle
Burning bright
I see your short, stout light.

Joshua Allen (10)
All Saints' CE Junior School

A Candle

The candlelight is fragile,
Its reflection shines out bright,
Flickers in the wind,
The little light has gone.

Light so bright -
You struggled, a fight -
But why did you go tonight?

Shadows dark and mean,
You're my only friend.
You - the light,
Illuminating the room.

Chloe Setchfield (10)
All Saints' CE Junior School

A Candle Poem

Flicker, flicker
Does it go,
Dancing, dancing, to and fro.
Candle, candle
Give your light,
Please don't blow out
In the night.
Brightly, brightly
A fiery shine,
All the candles in a line.

Making shadows
On the wall,
Standing elegant and tall!
Colourful candle
Blazing out,
All alone, short and stout.
Stops you having
A terrible fright,
Instead of darkness,
There is light.

Mariam Yaqoob (10)
All Saints' CE Junior School

A Candle

Flicker, flicker, goes the light,
In the cold, winter night.
A candle's bluish blaze,
I see you throughout the nights and days.
Candlelight, like a dream,
As it burns like a beam.
Candle so bright,
Flickering left and right.

Jacob Gould (10)
All Saints' CE Junior School

A Candle

Dancing
Darting
Flickering through the night,
Dancing
Darting
Giving a warm, glowing light.

Prancing
Darting
A blurry candle glimmers,
Prancing
Darting
The flame sparkles and shimmers.

Dancing
Prancing
Oh, how the candle does shine,
Dancing
Prancing
Accompanying me while I dine.

Prancing
Dancing
The candle is now just a spark,
Prancing
Dancing
Disappearing elegantly.

Emily Moore (11)
All Saints' CE Junior School

A Candle

Beautiful, beautiful,
Candle so bright,
I see you through,
The dark winter night.

Beautiful, beautiful,
Candle so bright,
I feel the warmth,
Coming from your light.

Beautiful, beautiful,
Candle so bright,
Your dancing brings,
The room to life.

Hannah Lamonte (10)
All Saints' CE Junior School

A Candle

Beautiful candle burning bright,
Keep that flame all through the night.

I see your shadows,
Dancing on the wall,
Stay by my side until morning is born.

Your light glimmers,
You stay awake,
Burning brightly,
And then,
You die away.

Rebekah Lawrence (10)
All Saints' CE Junior School

A Candle

Blazing
Gleaming
The candle glows
In the cold winter night.

Shining
Glistening
The candle glows
Reflecting itself on the table top.

Colourful
Fiery
The candle glows
Making shadows on the walls.

Fatima Shah (10)
All Saints' CE Junior School

A Candle

A candle has an egg-shaped flame,
A candle with its small, white flame,
A candle with its flame making a star on the table,
A candle with its flickering flame.

A candle has a bright, blazing flame,
A candle has a radiant, dancing flame,
A candle makes shadows move,
A candle has a short, pointed flame.

A candle dying,
A candle dying,
A candle dying.

Matthew Davis (10)
All Saints' CE Junior School

A Candle

A glowing flame,
A gleam so bright,
There it stands,
In a pool of light.

Shorter, taller,
In and out,
Sometimes it's tall,
Sometimes it's stout.

Flickering, dancing,
Side to side,
Swaying in the breeze,
As if trying to hide.

Onto dark walls,
Shadows are cast,
For the cold, dark night,
I wish you would last.

But now the flame dies,
There goes the warm light,
And now the room is dark and cold,
Oh please come back tomorrow night.

Rebecca Adamson (10)
All Saints' CE Junior School

Mirror World

I look into a mirror and all I see,
Is just beautiful simplicity,
Of the mirror girl, much better than me,
I touch her warm face gently,
She just stares right back at me.

Poor girl, she must be bored with me,
Her fingers touching innocently,
Why can't she swap places with me?
She's just a little girl I see,
Just like hurt, old damaged me.

I could stand here for all of the day,
Wishing I were her in mirror world,
I hope my wish does come true,
It would be such an honour to live like you,
With no rules or violence, oh yes it would.

In your world, I would be living like a queen,
With such a change from life over here,
With lots of dreams of course,
Because in my world of horror,
They're all that matter to me.

Lucy Skerritt (11)
Coates Community Primary School

The Sand And The Sea

The sand and the sea,
Whistle beautifully.
The sand and the sea,
Sparkle lovingly.
But as a chilly breeze comes over me,
I shiver in my step.
The sea settles down into its reef,
As does the sand into its depth.
A day has ended peacefully,
As I step down the path,
I walk with my memory.

Robin Hutchinson (11)
Coates Community Primary School

The War

War is here, I feel very frightened,
People, children crying for peace.
I'm all alone,
Got no family, just all alone.
I feel so lonely,
No one to talk to.
I'm dressed a boy, all alone,
Lots of people crying and dying.
People getting arms and legs chopped off.
I'm all alone in hiding.
Soon they will find me.
Shall I run away or stay and die?
The fire so hot, horrible sounds and smoke,
When will it fade?
Is this a dream or reality?
I hope it's a dream, so when I wake up
Everything's back to normal.
All I can do is pray to God,
I'm just a child in this despair and agony.
Please help me!

Kasim Shariq (11)
Fulbridge Junior School

Summer

Summer comes
    With the birds singing
Summer comes
    With the flowers blooming
Summer comes
    With bees buzzing
Summer comes
    With people swimming
Summer comes
    With people surfboarding
Summer comes
    With artists drawing
Summer comes
    With leopards running
Summer comes
    With people playing
Summer comes
    With butterflies fluttering.

Fashiha Ashiq (9)
Fulbridge Junior School

Rabbits

I am something that is very cuddly,
I am as cuddly as a teddy bear.

I am something that likes carrots,
I am as cute as parrots.

I am something that has big ears,
I am something that has no tears.

I am something that has goofy teeth,
I have tiny paws underneath.

So what am I?

Kiran Rashid (9)
Fulbridge Junior School

Young Writers - Once Upon A Rhyme Cambridgeshire

Rainbow Garden

Red the rose that blooms on a prickly bush,
The bloody poppy with the ebony centre,
The bright, luminous geranium
And the proud tulip which blooms in the spring.

Orange is the dahlia with its pompom head,
The dazzling tiger lily,
The fire-petalled nasturtium
And the fiery autumn leaves.

Yellow is the trumpet-like daffodil,
The tall standing sunflower, a stately plant,
The cheeky little buttercup
And the poached egg plant.

Green is the lime-coloured lady's mantle,
The spidery leaves of the yucca,
The shade-loving fern
And the round leaves of the water lily.

Blue is the tiny forget-me-not,
The frilly delphinium,
The sweet-smelling hyacinth
And the bluebells that chime in the woodland.

Pink is the silvery-leaved carnation,
The Chinese magnolia,
The nodding anemone
And the shocking-pink nerine.

Purple is the tumbling sweet pea,
The monkey-faced pansy,
The creeping clematis
And the calming lavender.

Oh! I love the rainbow garden!
With flowers that bloom all year round.

Ceri Pollard (9)
Fulbridge Junior School

Animal Jump

Leap like a leopard
Hop like a kangaroo
From branch to branch
Like a monkey in a zoo

Laugh like a hyena
Jump like a rabbit
Roar like a lion
You've got a bad habit

Slither like a snake
Fast like a cheetah
Bark like a dog
You've got the wrong heater

Eat like a lioness
Squeak like a mouse
Miaow like a cat
Keep away from the house

Build a web just like me
Flies get stuck
Like fairy puffs
I'm stuck in mud.

Shannon Zajac (8)
Fulbridge Junior School

Leap Like A Leopard

Leap like a leopard,
Hop like a kangaroo,
Swing from branch to branch,
Like a monkey in a zoo.

Sprint like a cheetah,
Jump like a cat,
Spin like a spider,
Hang like a bat.

Camouflage like a chameleon,
Bite like a shark,
Prowl like a lion,
Let your dog bark.

Run like an antelope,
Slither like a snake,
Fly like a bird,
Always be awake.

Daniel Baillie (9)
Fulbridge Junior School

Leap Like A Leopard

Leap like a leopard,
Hop like a kangaroo,
Swing from branch to branch,
Like a monkey in a zoo.

Purr like a cat,
Bark like a dog,
Roar like a lion,
'Ribbit' like a frog.

Cheep like a chicken,
Run like a hare,
Swim like a shark,
Growl like a bear.

Emma Henchman (8)
Fulbridge Junior School

Winter

Winter comes
    With snow falling
Winter comes
    With morning icy
Winter comes
    With festival celebrating
Winter comes
    With people sneaking
Winter comes
    With snowflake falling
Winter comes
    With ice breaking
Winter comes
    With decoration shining
Winter comes
    With people eating
Winter comes
    With breezes freezing
Winter comes
    With wind breaking.

Rumaanah Raqeeb (8)
Fulbridge Junior School

Kitty Party

At school we had an awful test
So after that we got dressed
It was Sofie's birthday
That's now in May
So we did put on make-up and got dressed.

Soon we were as comfortable as a bird in its nest
Us, Nelly and Beth went to town
We bought Sofie a golden crown
We made a superb make
Of a perfect, fantastic chocolate cake.

We set up the food
Everyone was in a really good mood
We danced all night
In the disco light
All us good mates
We all shared and ate
Until it was time to go home
In the morning we went to the Millennium Dome.

Heena Saleem (10)
Fulbridge Junior School

Mattie

M attie is the best,
A nd better than the rest,
T o everyone he's a geek,
T o me he's lovely and sweet,
I think he's really hunky,
E ven though he looks quite funky.

Jessica Trower (11)
Fulbridge Junior School

The Dark

I don't like the dark coming down on my head,
It feels like a blanket thrown over the bed.
I don't like the dark coming down on my head.

I don't like the dark coming down over me,
It feels like the room's full of things I can't see.
I don't like the dark coming down over me.

There isn't enough light from under the door,
It only just reaches the floor.
There isn't enough light from under the door.

I wish my dad hadn't put out the light,
It feels like there's something out of sight.
I wish my dad hadn't put out the light.

But under the bedclothes it's warm and secure,
You can't see the ceiling, you can't see the floor.
Yes, under the bedclothes it's nice and secure,
So I think I'll stay here till it's daylight once more.

Daniel Wright (10)
Fulbridge Junior School

The Poem Of The World!

The world became polite, nice and kind,
When all the tribes in the land lived in peace:

There were no wars among them,
Summer was always in the air,
The streams were clear and pure
And filled with fish.

Birdsong rang the from every tree
And the earth was rich
With everything that people needed
In the world.

Saba Zia (9)
Fulbridge Junior School

Winter

Winter comes
>   With snowflakes sparkling
Winter comes
>   With robins singing
Winter comes
>   With fire burning
Winter comes
>   With snow tumbling
Winter comes
>   With fun sledging
Winter comes
>   With hot chocolate warming
Winter comes
>   With people visiting
Winter comes
>   With people skating
Winter comes
>   With presents opening.

Henna Sajjad (9)
Fulbridge Junior School

All About Mum

Mum is kind and sweet,
She is like a treat.

She makes me laugh
And have a bath!

She giggles and wriggles
And tickles and tickles.

She is smart
And has a very good heart.

I love her kiss,
She's the one I really miss.

Hina Iqbal (10)
Fulbridge Junior School

Winter Comes

Winter comes
     With people sledging
Winter comes
     With animals hibernating
Winter comes
     With winds flying
Winter comes
     With snowflakes sparkling
Winter comes
     With presents opening
Winter comes
     With dinners serving
Winter comes
     With snow spreading
Winter comes
     With excitement flowing
Winter comes
     With people sleeping.

Matthew Gentleman (9)
Fulbridge Junior School

Untitled

Sparkling madly the Roaring Rocket whistles loudly.
Bursting beautifully the firefighter sparkles and crackles gently.
Jumping fiercely the Jumping Jack sparkles silently.
Sparkling crazily the Mental Mandy growls viciously.
Smashing wildly the Dainty Dragon spits fire.
Fiercely smashing the Glitter Glamour throws devil's fire.

Asad Hussain (10)
Fulbridge Junior School

Night Comes

Night comes
    With stars twinkling
Night comes
    With bats flapping
Night comes
    With moon shining
Night comes
    With darkness growing
Night comes
    With cats fighting
Night comes
    With owls hunting
Night comes
    With people shouting
Night comes
    With dogs sleeping
Night comes
    With babies crying.

Waqas Hussain (8)
Fulbridge Junior School

Winter

Winter comes
    With snowballs flying
Winter comes
    With snowmen smiling
Winter comes
    With snow fairies laughing
Winter comes
    With partying
Winter comes
    With children playing
Winter comes
    With ice skating
Winter comes
    With cold trees whistling
Winter comes
    With the wind shaking
Winter comes
    With adults chasing.

Hassan Ahmed (8)
Fulbridge Junior School

Love!

Love, love, sweet love in the air for everyone,
No matter what anyone says,
Money can't bring you love,
No matter what you pay,
It's all from the heart.

Love, love, sweet love in the air,
Love brings you happiness and joy,
Forever and ever,
Love is not a toy,
It's real and brings you luck.

Love, love, sweet love in the air for everyone,
No matter what anyone says,
Money can't bring you love,
No matter what you pay,
It's all from the heart.

Kiran Kaur Sohi (11)
Fulbridge Junior School

There's A Monster In The Classroom

The children are happy in the playground,
Unaware of the danger lurking around,
They are all skipping to and fro,
Teacher calls, 'Come on class, in you go.'
All in line walking to class,
No one noticed the danger they passed,
Sitting down the children, Miss writing on the board,
Something so frightening cannot be ignored,
Outside the windows, colours orange, blue and green,
Shadow in the hallway was never seen,
Hard thumping steps faster and faster,
The class door flies open, oh my God!
        It's the *headmaster!*

Shelby Summers (11)
Fulbridge Junior School

My Sister

My sister has run away
I remember we used to fight
She left me here to deal with her problems
She's gone into the night

Why am I so down, Mother?
Why am I so sad?
We never used to get on
And now I'm feeling bad

I love her so much, Mother
I miss her lots
Even though we used to fight
Getting hair in knots

Why did she run away, Mother?
I heard a voice at night
Is it something to do with me?
It also gave me a fright!

I hope she comes back, Mother
I promise we won't fight
Why did she have to run away
In the middle of the night?

I want her back now, Mother
It's already the month of May
Oh look over there, Mother
She's back today!

Sehrish Ahmed (9)
Fulbridge Junior School

Anger

Anger is very powerful,
He's a rich coal-black,
He burns you with fiery flames,
He's a killer's worst attack!

Anger consumes your happy thoughts,
Leaving them with terrible fears,
Leaving them with nasty hatred,
Envy and sometimes tears!

Your teeth gritted together,
Your fists clenched really tight,
Your heart racing and leaping,
He makes you want to fight!

Your muscles tighten fiercely,
He makes you really mad,
You want to yell and scream at him,
And make him feel bad!

Rukhsaar Ali (11)
Fulbridge Junior School

The Always Working Tree

The tree sings in the wind, the branches hitting,
grabbing at each other.
Roots are tunnelling in the wet, muddy ground
searching for water.
Branches waving, stretching, high leaves falling down,
tumbling as well.
The trunk posing, bending on one leg,
Bark rough and wrinkly in the wind.
The tree sweats in the sun as it works so hard
to find water in the ground.
Leaves moving to catch the light of the lazy sun in the day.

Keipher Ormesher (10)
Gunthorpe Primary School

The Personality Of Winter

All the animals in the world
Are hiding from the cold
Winter has crept up on us
But nature cannot be controlled.

A hedgehog's hiding in the leaves
Fed up with all the snow
The trees are whispering in the wind
And a snowman is on show.

All the animals in the world
Are hiding from the cold
Winter has crept up on us
But nature cannot be controlled.

A squirrel is climbing up a tree
And birds flying to their nest
The cat is sleeping on the sofa
Which he thinks is the best.

All the animals in the world
Are hiding from the cold
Winter has crept up on us
But nature cannot be controlled.

The pond is frozen because of the snow
And the birds are in their little house
The snowflakes are darting down to earth
And don't forget the poor little mouse.

All the animals in the world
Are hiding from the cold
Winter has crept up on us
But nature cannot be controlled.

The snow is keeping the Earth's crust warm
Because it thinks it is a quilt
I really am quite surprised
That winter doesn't feel any guilt.

All the animals in the world
Are hiding from the cold
Winter has crept up on us
But nature cannot be controlled.

Daniel Twinn-Waters (11)
Gunthorpe Primary School

Spider's Oak

The tree on the side of the forest, the sap oozing.
The roots turning under the flat, wet earth.
I can hear it talking, whistling and waving, it is too much.
I run through the grass to find it's still there.
I know it's searching for moisture.
I never should have drunk my drink in front of a tree.
For a start, I should never have chosen water.
I can hear the roots digging, sucking, gurgling.
It's somewhere in this overgrown jungle, turning over the land!

The tree's getting smaller and smaller.
I can see it swaying and stretching.
I'm glad I'm not under the tree still.
It's shooting the fallen branches at me.
It's snowing, hoorah! I can throw snowballs.
I put a stone in one and throw it.
The tree starts crying.
Then all spiders start to come out.
There are all sorts.
The winter season just got colder!

Ryan Launchbury (9)
Gunthorpe Primary School

Winter Is Here

As the darkness creeps over the light
Birds with angel wings fly in delight
Squirrels dash this way and that
To locate the warmth to habitat
Animals must ration their food
The snowman looks like he's in a good mood.

Pond life never sees the sky until spring
The magpies look for a shiny thing
Inside, the cat
Sleeps on the mat
We sit by the fire
Listening for the choir
To melt the icicles growing on my fingertips
We eat away to our chocolate dips.

Snuggled in my bed
A thought comes to my head
About Christmas.

Ashley Newstead (10)
Gunthorpe Primary School

Autumn Leaves

Autumn leaves drifting through the air,
As they touch the ground so fair,
Orange, yellow, gold and red,
All these colours the tree has shed,
Crisp and crunchy on the floor,
Making piles outside the door,
Winter frost will soon be here,
Which means the start of a new year.

Charlie Kingston (9)
Gunthorpe Primary School

My Valentine

I sit in class and stare,
At a boy with brown hair.
He has brown eyes,
In my dreams he lies.
He's scruffy and he's gorgeous,
But to go near would be dangerous.

He doesn't love me, but I love him,
It's time to admit that Cupid's been.
He's my valentine forever,
We got it going together.
You're a dream come true,
If you go with me I won't feel blue.
You're my valentine!

Sophie Knight (9)
Gunthorpe Primary School

The Tree

An old, bent tree, with roots stiff and hollow,
The rain comes and smashes on the trunk,
Bending it even more to the ground.
The branches twist and swirl
As the leaves fall down, tumbling and fidgeting.
Branches huddle together as the rain comes,
Sap bleeding quickly out of the tree.
All the bark's wrinkled and rusted.
Every day the roots slurp up through the trunk
And into the thirsty twigs and branches.

Ainsley Robertson (10)
Gunthorpe Primary School

The Trees In The Wood

It was a windy day in the woods
The tree was singing beautifully
And its twigs were twitching and waving
And whistling to the wind
Talking to all the leaves flying past
Sharing secrets that are never to be found
Conkers being dropped on you
Wondering what is going to be dropped on you next
Go further and you will see trees shivering and shaking
Whistling deeper in the forest
Standing as still as a building.

Callum Bowyer (9)
Gunthorpe Primary School

Blue Is . . .

The sea crashing against the rocks.
My purse lying in my bag.
A bluebell swaying in the wind.
Bluebirds feeding worms to their young.
A book waiting to be written in.
A swimming pool that I am splashing in.
Blueberry juice waiting to be drunk.

Stacey Cann (10)
Gunthorpe Primary School

The Tall Tree

Its trunk standing stiff and tall,
Growing right up into the sunlight.
Its roots twirling and digging down into the crispy ground,
Searching for water.
The leaves dancing in the wind
And swaying side to side in the light breeze.

Natasha Stones (9)
Gunthorpe Primary School

The Trees Of The Wood

Watching the tree sway in the wind,
An old oak tree, its roots tough and hard.
Crispy, waving at me as if it knows me,
Its leaves fidgeting in the wind.
The tree's whistling,
Telling secrets that nobody knows.
The chainsaw comes near,
It's weeping.
It's going to be made into paper.
Goodbye trees.

Daniel Smith (9)
Gunthorpe Primary School

Blue Is . . .

A bluebell waving slowly in the woods.
Waves crashing madly against the rocks.
A butterfly fluttering in the sky.
A bluebird singing softly in the tree.
The sky with the sun and clouds sitting in the distance.
My bedcovers waiting for me to snuggle up in.
A book waiting for me to read it.

Chloe Frisby (10)
Gunthorpe Primary School

The Amazing Catherine Wheel

The fire getting ready, the food looking good,
Almost time to see the stars and colours.
Crack, sizzle, pop went the sparklers.
They were all counting down, nothing happened.
Bang!
Went the Catherine wheel.

Olivia Gourlay (10)
Gunthorpe Primary School

My Dad

My dad's sometimes sad,
My dad's sometimes glad,
My dad does not get cross,
My dad says he's the boss,
My dad makes me smile,
My dad plays a while,
My dad beats me at chess,
My dad's just the best.

Samantha Burns (9)
Gunthorpe Primary School

Dragons

D readful fire-breathing beasts
R aged skin as tough as nails
A vast race of evil beasts
G igantic terror-winged beasts spread fear
O nly dragons breathe fire
N ever will you come across these fine beasts
S ome don't breathe fire, but water.

Jake Moore (9)
Gunthorpe Primary School

Gold Is . . .

A coin spinning on the table
A golden ticket glittering in the wrapper
My gold coins shining in the sun
A golden football cup glowing in the sun
A ring twisting on my finger.

Jake Church (9)
Gunthorpe Primary School

Cars Racing, Cars Chasing

Cars racing, cars chasing
All around, but they stay on the ground.
Cars racing, cars chasing,
When they all come round the corner,
Blue, black, white, pink and yellow
All side by side.
Cars racing, cars chasing,
Who's going to win?
Who's going to win?

Nathan Setchfield (9)
Gunthorpe Primary School

Gold Is . . .

A necklace jingling around my neck
A beautiful ring shining on my little finger
A bracelet twisting around my wrist
A football rolling around my feet
A coin dropping in my purse
A watch telling me the time
A trophy sparkling in my hands
A firework going round and round.

Nicole Duffy (9)
Gunthorpe Primary School

Fireworks

Pop! Oh, there it goes again!
Pop, bang, crackle, crash!
It's very loud, then it goes *bash!*
The colours it has, they're so beautiful,
Red, orange and yellow.
It whizzes up so high into the sky,
But then it spins round like a Catherine wheel.
Then it dies off and that's the end of it.

Hannah Cooper (9)
Gunthorpe Primary School

The Moon

A silver penny tossed high into the
twinkling quilt of the sky.

Tattered rag clouds blow gently across the
softly shining circle of cheese.

A ghostly silver pancake flung into a
net of thrashing branches.

A small pearl rolling slowly along a black tarmac road,
the puddles of clouds drift by.

Hettie Davies (10)
John Clare Primary School

My Kennings

Milk licker
Wool catcher
Window watcher
Bed rester
Bird chaser
Leaves player
Jelly eater
Long dreamer
Crafty cat!

Evangeline Rata (9)
John Clare Primary School

The Stars

Inside one pitch-black galaxy,
The shining stars were born.
Some stars were hot
And some were not.
Then came the biggest star of all,
The sun, the brightest of them all.

Tara Lepore (7)
John Clare Primary School

The Land Of Make-Believe

In the land where the leprechauns play
And fierce fire-breathing lizards are slayed
By knights in shining armour so bold
In tales that are amazingly old.
Commanded by kings with hundreds of rings
Whose sons marry beautiful peasants
And dine in the palace on pheasants.
While witches, hags and enchantresses
In awfully dirty, brown dresses
Lean over a cauldron so black
In tall, crumpled, crooked hats
Reading their spell books so thick
Whilst stirring a poison that spits.
Meanwhile, dwarves mine rubies in holes
But normally end up with coal!
Princes rescue maidens in towers
From wizards with magical powers
And run for a day to a castle far away
And live happily ever after!

Ethan Brooks (10)
John Clare Primary School

Kennings Henry VIII

Party lover
Boar hunter
Meat devourer
Church splitter
Death caster
Multiple marrier
Music player
Wife slayer -
Henry VIII.

Angharad Davies (9)
John Clare Primary School

School Bus

There goes the bell, now starts the journey of Hell.
Children bawling,
Others crawling,
Throwing stones at others' bones.
Cracked windows, broken nose,
One child wanted to be caged,
Another screamed, 'The toilet's engaged!'
Someone wanted bubblegum,
The baby at the front is sucking his thumb.
Down the aisle having a race,
Is little Billy with a rather red face.
Someone screamed, 'The tyre's flat!'
The teacher passed away on the mat.
The children thought there was an earthquake,
Fat old Tommy spilt his milkshake!
Now the journey's come to an end,
It will drive anyone round the bend!

Olivia Fricker (9)
John Clare Primary School

The Cat

Hiding under the blanket
Miaow! Out comes the cat.

Eyes gleaming wickedly
Then jumps on my aunt's best hat.

Purring like a steam engine
Knowing that's a naughty deed.

I put his food down on the floor
Then he eats it up with greed.

The cat sits there innocently
Desperate to be found.

He looks just like an impatient king
Waiting to be crowned.

Jessica Bradley (10)
John Clare Primary School

Kennings

Earth cracker
Floor breaker

Rubble bringer
House taker

Natural thunderer
Heart breaker

Death bringer
Family splitter

Earthquake!

George Wilson (11)
John Clare Primary School

Kennings

Slow mover,
Lazy sleeper,
Leaf eater,
Fruit nibbler,
Rainforest inhabitor,
Branch clinger,
Tree climber,
Good swimmer.

I'm a sloth!

Amelia Markham (11)
John Clare Primary School

Haiku

Blood-red scavenger
A violently scratching claw
Dark woodland dweller.

Leo Rytina (10)
John Clare Primary School

Spider

Lurking in the bathtub
Lurking in your room
Lurking under sofas
They're coming out soon.
Some are big
Some are small
Some are short
Some are tall.
Some are hairy
Some are fat
Some are skinny
Some are flat.
There are different kinds of spiders
They have different sizes of webs
Waiting for their dinner
They're coming out soon.

Scott Roberts (8)
John Clare Primary School

Animals

Big animals,
Small animals,
Animals all around.
Scaly animals,
Soft animals,
Animals on the land.
Water animals,
Earth animals,
Animals up in trees.
Fierce animals,
Sweet animals,
Animals scuttering around.
Noisy animals,
Quiet animals,
Animals all over the world.

Jessica Shaw (8)
John Clare Primary School

At Night

It's strange
But the
Moment
I turn out
My
Light
I
Get
Frightened
By the
Things
That go
Bump in
The night.
I hear
Crackle, crackle,
Crackle
And a *slam*
From the
Door.
I hear
Thump, thump,
Thump
From the
Floor.
Oh,
It's
My
Dad!

Kelly Stockwell (8)
John Clare Primary School

World War II

The war is tough
Hitler is very rough
The soldiers will march into battle.

The war is tough
Germans are rough
We battle for our lives.

The war is tough
Hitler is very rough
The battle is not over.

The war is tough
Germans are very rough
We will never give up.

The war is tough
Hitler is very rough
All the people will fight.

The war is tough
Germans are very rough
We will shoot all of them.

The war is tough
Hitler is very rough
We have beaten them.

The war is tough
Germans are very rough
We have nearly won.

The war is tough
Hitler is very rough
Hitler will soon die.

Britain are winning
Germany are losing
We have victory.

Lewis Jackson (9)
John Clare Primary School

Sunrise

When I look out my window
On a nice summer morning,
I spot the sunrise.
I say, 'Mum, look at the sunrise.'
The pleasant, golden sun
So glossy and bright.
The beautiful colours
So pale and cool.
Sunrise is my favourite time of morning.

Emily Seaton (9)
John Clare Primary School

World War II

War is a time for fighting and explosions
and bombs are coming down.
I have a feeling we're gonna get bombed,
so go in your shelter and don't come out
until the sirens go off again.
When it's all clear, then come out of your shelter
and go to your home.
Now you are safe and sound.

Molly Webster (8)
John Clare Primary School

River

Stone carver
Quick mover
Long faller
Fast flow-er
Mountain starter
Large flooder
Bank eroder
Rock pusher.

Hugh Markham (9)
John Clare Primary School

Motorcycling Jack

I'm motorcycling Jack,
I'm so cool,
The girls at school,
Whistle as I go past.
Me girlfriend's a rock chick,
Me mum's so wick.
Me dad's a fighter,
I wonder what I might be
As I grow old just like he!
I grease me hair with engine oil,
Me cat and dog are called Crab and Goil.
Her bright yellow eyes,
Her big burnished lips,
As she rips my heart out
Like a fly with a spark.

Hannah Morton (9)
John Clare Primary School

Bump In The Night

While I lie in bed
I hear noises.
I hear *knock, knock, knock.*
I imagine that Frankenstein
Is knocking on my door before I wake,
'Let me in, let me in.'

Every night I hear noises.
I hear *tick, tick, tick.*
I like scaring myself, so I do.
I think that the Grim Reaper
Is breaking my door down.

Jason Grandidge (8)
John Clare Primary School

Dragons

Dragons black, white and grey,
Flashing flames light the day.
Dragons both far and near,
Very easy to see clear.
Dragons swim, dragons fly,
Dragons fly across the sky.
Dragons fierce, dragons bad,
Dragons are very mad.
Dragons roar, dragons squeak,
Dragons are very sweet.

Hayley White (9)
John Clare Primary School

World War II

Bombs dropping,
Sirens bleeping,
Children screaming,
Mothers hiding,
Evacuees say goodbye,
Planes fly around the sky,
Trains chug along the track,
Children being whipped on the back,
Every time I go to sleep,
I think how terrible war was.

Jemima Davies (7)
John Clare Primary School

Tree

On
top
of the
emerald
green, sparkling
tree there stood a gleaming, glossy,
glittering, gold *star* dazzling away. It's her job.
The tree is green,
the tree is
sparkling,
the tree
is
always
out at Christmas.
Tinsel, tinsel, leaping, lolloping
around.
Red
pot
sturdy pot
holding the
tree, the tinsel,
the star.

Lindsey Irons (9)
John Clare Primary School

Electricity

Shooting through the wires like a ball flying in the sky,
Going over fields and underground in cities,
Whizzing like a racing car at 100 miles per hour.
It's spinning round and round, it's going to villages,
It's slowing down now, it's reaching the village.
It's in the house and has settled down in a lamp.

Leo Davies (7)
John Clare Primary School

Cats

Cats eat anything,
from mice and rats,
to a pile of string!

Grass, plants, buzzy bees,
rabbits, hamsters,
bark from trees!

Chicken, ducks, cows and mice,
leather shoes,
and plastic dice.

Harriet Warren (11)
John Clare Primary School

If . . .

(Based on 'If' by Rudyard Kipling)

If I can defend my territory without conceding a single goal,
If I can keep my cool when players rant and rave,
If I can keep my head high when we lose a goal,
If I can show signs of sportsmanship when the opposing team do not,
If I can concentrate on the game and blank out the screaming

of parents,
If I can score a goal and not boast.
If I can respect the ref's decision without any strain,
If I can not taunt players about my winning,
If I can head the ball without fretting,
If I can be friendly to the opposing team, yet still play my best,
Then I would be the most amazing footballer.

Keanu Parkinson (10)
Leighton Primary School

If . . .

(Based on 'If' by Rudyard Kipling)

If I could sing better I'd sing everywhere
If I could practise more I'd be better at games
If I could write on no guidelines, it would be easy to read my writing
If I could keep my hand in the air and wait, instead of putting it down,
I will be picked more often
If I could not be bossy to my sister and friends, I would probably get
more friends,
If I could keep on trying to be better and good, I would probably get
some money and help my mum buy some food
If I could sit with a straight back in class all the time, then I would be
happy and helpful for everyone, even my friends, and I would be a
healthy adult.

Chelsea Budden (9)
Leighton Primary School

If . . .

(Based on 'If' by Rudyard Kipling)

If I could sit up in class for hours,
If I could draw a straight line in maths without a ruler,
If I could write neatly in literacy,
If I could spell my words right in stories,
If I could write beautifully in all lessons,
If I could not make as many mistakes in my books,
If I could make more friends when I move playgrounds,
If I could get all my spellings right every week,
If I could remember to do my homework before Thursday night,
If I could remember my PE kit every Monday and Friday,
Then my school day will be perfect.

Samantha Longman
Leighton Primary School

If . . .

(Based on 'If' by Rudyard Kipling)

If you can swim without sinking,
If you can do backstroke without stopping,
If you can succeed without boasting,
If you can breaststroke without kicking someone,
If you can dive into the pool and feel the water running through
your hair,
If you can do without quitting,
If you can try without being heartless,
If you can struggle without losing your head,
If you can swim without showing off,
If you can make decisions without shouting,
Then you will be an adult, my girl.

Bethany Hawes (10)
Leighton Primary School

If . . .

(Based on 'If' by Rudyard Kipling)

If I can finish my maths before time is up,
If I can get 20 spellings right without looking in a dictionary,
If I can do PE without going wrong or falling over,
If I can swim without drowning,
If I can play outside without being hit or pushed over,
If I can do literacy without going wrong,
If I can ask for help when I am stuck and in a pickle,
If I can listen to Mr Ward in science without talking,
If I can eat my dinner without dropping it down my top,
If I can stay strong and do my homework without losing my head,
Then my day would be perfect.

Xeña Howlett (11)
Leighton Primary School

If . . .

(Based on 'If' by Rudyard Kipling)

If I could concentrate on my game and ignore the shouting of
parents telling me what to do,
If I could dive further and keep Leighton in the game again,
If I could set up a one-on-one for someone and not make
them offside,
If I could keep my temper and agree with the ref and not
get a card,
If I could do big kicks and not give it to the opposition,
If I could encourage my teammates and keep our hopes up,
If I could organize my defence and not let the other team have
as many shots,

If I could keep my marker and not drift,
If I could take my free kicks and score,
If I could run the ball up and down the pitch,
Then I'll be a footie master.

Declan Higgins (10)
Leighton Primary School

If . . .

(Based on 'If' by Rudyard Kipling)

If I can do a test and just try my best,
If I can accomplish an entire page of work, then add a bit of brain
to give a little jerk,
If I can triumph in numeracy, I'll try the same in literacy,
If I can keep my cool, then in science I will rule,
If I can win in PE,
If I can stay calm while others are arguing,
If I can complete my work in the time given,
If I could swim a length, my teacher would be proud of me,
If I can do Jet, I could show my teacher a thing or two,
If I can do all these things, I'll succeed in school.

Norton Crowson (11)
Leighton Primary School

If . . .

(Based on 'If' by Rudyard Kipling)

If I could play football without falling over,
The other team would have less chance of scoring a goal.
If I could keep the ball on the pitch,
I would be able to play better.
If I could pass the ball to people,
We might be able to score a goal.
If I could hit the ball harder,
That will be a big improvement.
If I could not talk to people on the sideline,
I could play a lot better.
If I would concentrate,
I might be able to make it into the football team.
If I could get changed quicker,
Then nobody would have to wait for me.
If I wouldn't talk at half-time,
I wouldn't get told off.
If I wouldn't stand still on the pitch,
I might be Man of the Match.

Jonathan Kingston (9)
Leighton Primary School

If . . .

(Based on 'If' by Rudyard Kipling)

If I could work without talking to my friend next door,
If I could sharpen a pencil without it ending up with no lead,
If I could paint without it going everywhere,
If I could sit with my back straight and not slope down,
If I could write without it going slanted,
If I could read without stopping to spell a word out,
If I could hand my homework in on time every week,
If I could learn my spellings and know them off by heart,
If I could sing in assembly without hitting a wrong note,
If I could swim without panicking,
Then I will do well at school and hopefully one day become
a teacher.

Rosie Horton-Williams (10)
Leighton Primary School

If . . .

(Based on 'If' by Rudyard Kipling)

If I could try my best in life and still get it wrong
it wouldn't matter.
If I could play football and not get picked last
or get in the way.
If I could keep my top on when I'm joking around
with my friends.
If I could sit through assembly
without fidgeting.
If I could stand level with my friends
instead of looking up to them.
If I could make a promise
without breaking it.
If I could know my spellings
and not be a class clown.
If I could sit through a lesson
without talking.
If I could swim in my own side of the pool
and stay with my group.
If I could go five minutes
without making a comment . . .

Andrew O'Sullivan (10)
Leighton Primary School

Rugby Crazy Cinquain

Rugby
Mega challenge
Jogging, scoring, falling
Making lots of tries in the sun
Jonny.

Aaron Lowey (9)
Leighton Primary School

The Feeling Poem

I love the feel of . . .
The soft, silky fur
On a dazzling Dalmatian
Who lives down my street.

I love the feel of . . .
Newly cut, short hair
Curling cutely round my ears.

I hate the feel of . . .
Scaly, slimy fish
When I'm swimming
Swiftly in the sea.

I hate the feel of . . .
Scratchy, salty sand
As I walk across the beach
It goes through my toes
It stays there forever.

Georgina Amey (10)
Leighton Primary School

If . . .

(Based on 'If' by Rudyard Kipling)

If I could practise every day without giving up after a missed shot,
If I could agree with the ref before getting stressed,
If I could pass every ball before I get tackled,
If I could defend my territory without conceding a goal,
If I could keep mentally strong in every game,
If I could play my best in every match,
If I could be friends with my teammates and not fall out,
If I could help the manager through bad times,
If I could take long throws without lifting my foot,
If I could win trophies and not boast,
Then I would be the world's best footballer.

Christopher Greenacre (11)
Leighton Primary School

If . . .

(Based on 'If' by Rudyard Kipling)

If you can feel the music but still be relaxed,
If you can cleoshai and still keep a straight back,
If you can work with the rest of your team and not lose your head
                when others are if something goes wrong,
If you can get the sequence right and not stare at others who cannot,
If you can point your toe and keep a straight leg whilst doing so,
If you can accept not being chosen for the part and try again
                next time,
If you can manage to perform and special part on stage and be
                without fright,
If you can jump and spin in the air and not fall,
If you can be the star without being boastful,
If you can bend down to touch your toes without straining,
Then you will be a dancer, my child.

Christle Boyden (10)
Leighton Primary School

If . . .

(Based on 'If' by Rudyard Kipling)

If I can play on a football pitch and stay on my feet,
If I could get past defenders without the linesman seeing,
If I could get 100% shouting and cheering from the crowd,
If I can get my teammates to stop shouting at me and just play,
      even though sometimes they don't know what they're on about,
If I could shoot from distance and hit the crossbar without knocking
                the goalie out,
If I could take a free kick and curl it like the wind and break the net,
If I could do a fair tackle without hearing that whistle,
If I could sprint back to defence and block the shot,
If I could run up and down without getting a stitch,
Then I could be a professional footballer.

Ben Syder (10)
Leighton Primary School

Tasty Poem

I love the taste of . . .
Creamy fudge tart
Melting in my mouth
With smooth, creamy custard.

I hate the taste of . . .
Boiled Brussel sprouts
The smell gets right up my nose
And makes me gag as it travels down my mouth.

I love the taste of . . .
Dairy Milk smooth, brown chocolate
In a shiny, silvery wrapper
Melting in my mouth.

I hate the taste of . . .
Sizzling hot dogs
In crispy, crunchy buns
With hot, yellow mustard.
                    Yuck!

Clare McGrath (10)
Leighton Primary School

If . . .

(Based on 'If' by Rudyard Kipling)

If I can conquer primary school without a problem,
If I can battle against secondary school without a doubt,
If I can defeat sixth form without a puzzle,
If I can complete college without difficulty,
If I can fulfill university without a dilemma,
If I can become a vet without any trouble,
If I can proclaim my duty without a complication,
If I can save animals without a predicament,
If I can help creatures without giving them pain,
If I can get through my life without any trouble,
Then I have become a successful woman!

Georgia Paul (11)
Leighton Primary School

If . . .

(Based on 'If' by Rudyard Kipling)

If I can keep calm and not lose my head
If I can concentrate on my work and not be misled
If I can keep my writing neat and always do my best
If I can succeed in numeracy, I'll try with the rest
If I pass my test, I will not gloat
If I triumph in the playground, I will not boast
If I get a star for excellent work
If I don't get picked, I'll try next time
If I am writing a poem, I'll try to make it rhyme
If I behave in assembly, my teacher will be proud of me,
Then I will be a good pupil.

Molly Edgar (10)
Leighton Primary School

If . . .

(Based on 'If' by Rudyard Kipling)

If I could keep my cool when others accuse me,
If I could respect everyone, when all they do is moan and shout,
If I could have my own opinion, but listen to others,
If I could play with my friends and not end up in tears,
If I could listen to what my parents say without getting angry,
If I could defend my friends, but not get involved too much,
If I could walk away from fights when others carry on,
If I could share all my toys without keeping the toys to myself,
If I could keep a secret close to my heart,
Then I would be the greatest friend that anyone could want.

Farah Anverkhan (11)
Leighton Primary School

If . . .

(Based on 'If' by Rudyard Kipling)

If I can work hard in school and achieve a great deal,
If I can go out in the playground and make new friends,
If I can sit up straight and not fall back,
If I can say sorry to people I hurt,
If I can behave so well, I'll not be heard,
If I can go to school and not be stopped,
If I can sit all day and not be seen,
If I can try real hard and finish my work,
If I can say this to you, you can say it to me,
If I run really fast, then you can run along with me,
Then I will be successful at school and become a teacher.

Alexandra Doyle (9)
Leighton Primary School

If . . .

(Based on 'If' by Rudyard Kipling)

If I can use my mind and not my mouth
If I can sit up straight and not fall down
If I can run around all day long
If I can do my work without making a sound
If I can make new friends that won't let me down
If I can talk to you and listen carefully
If I can do well in sport and not be put down
If I can behave in class but still have a laugh
If I can read all day and remember the story too
If I can play outside and not get hurt
    Then I'll survive school.

Victoria Cartledge (9)
Leighton Primary School

If . . .

(Based on 'If' by Rudyard Kipling)

If I can sit with my back straight for hours
I will have a straight back forever,
If I can write my handwriting in straight lines
I will have neat work,
If I can be sensible in the playground
I will not get into trouble so much.
If I can swim perfectly
I will never have to take swimming lessons forever,
If I can do my jobs perfectly
I will know how to work,
If I can write without my pencil breaking
I will not have to keep sharpening it,
If I can read without stopping to spell words
I will be brilliant at reading,
If I can write my spellings out knowing I am going to get 15
I will be an excellent spelling girl,
If I can hand my homework in on time
I will never have to stay in at break,
If I can do all these things
I will be a good adult.

Jemma Harber (10)
Leighton Primary School

Art

I am lovely and colourful,
I can do lots of splodging,
I can use lots of paint.
My pictures can look powerful,
I have different textures.
You can swirl the paint around on the paper,
We can make wonderful paintings.

Shannon Doyle (9)
Leighton Primary School

If . . .

(Based on 'If' by Rudyard Kipling)

If I could complete the day from start to finish,
If I could finish my work without my pencil breaking,
If I could at least get 19 out of 20 for mental maths,
If I could finish *all* my dinner before the bell goes,
If I could keep a smile on my face for the whole day,
If I could just keep cool for the last couple of hours,
If I could survive the day without getting detention,
If I could do my homework before the dog eats it,
If I could just try to improve at maths,
If I could keep as many friends as possible,
If I could succeed at this,
Then I could proudly get through my school year.

Louise Hooper (10)
Leighton Primary School

If . . .

(Based on 'If' by Rudyard Kipling)

If I can go on stage without getting scared,
If I can meet the stars without being embarrassed,
If I can control my nerves and enjoy myself thoroughly,
If I can be proud without being boastful,
If I can be determined about my career without changing my mind,
If I can be strong and never give in,
If I can love people whether they support me or not,
If people can care for me, even if they don't like what I do,
If I can remember my lines and say them clearly,
If I can do all of this,
Then I'll live my dream.

Alice Chapman (10)
Leighton Primary School

Kennings

Always - working
Everyone - muttering
People - thinking
Choir - singing
Teachers - shouting
Corridors - shutting
Light - flickering
Paper - cutting
Bells - ringing
Toilet - flushing
Taps - running
Drawers - opening
Books - falling
What am I?

Clare Foster (11)
Leighton Primary School

Kennings Art

Teacher - demonstrating
Paints - mixing
Paper - rustling
Pencils - drawing
Brushing - stroking
Children - concentrating
Scissors - cutting
Water - flicking
Pastels - colouring.
    What am I?

Jemma Horton (11)
Leighton Primary School

Love And Hate

I love the taste of . . .
Creamy, crunchy, white chocolate
In a sloppy, shimmering wrapper
Mouth-watering in my mouth.

I hate the taste of . . .
Covered in cream hot dogs
With a layer of brown ketchup
In a slimy, crispy bun.

I love the taste of . . .
Creamy, lovely cake
With a layer of icing sugar
Beautiful and gorgeous cake.

I hate the taste of . . .
Freezing ice cream
With a layer of chocolate
And a sloppy, slimy sauce.

I love the taste of . . .
Lovely, sweet pizza
With stretchy cheese and burning chillies.

Paul Barnes (11)
Leighton Primary School

School Life

I am a place where children work
I have twelve large rooms filled with tables and chairs
I have two large halls used for assembly, PE and dinner
Media suite built for children to use
Always chatting, playground filled with children
Office phones ringing, sound of keyboards tapping, bell ringing
                                    three times a day.

What am I?

Tamara Hole (10)
Leighton Primary School

The Love And Hate Poem

I love the taste of . . .
Lovely melted chocolate
With chunky toffee inside
Melting slowly into your mouth.

I love the taste of . . .
Lovely chunky duck with orange sauce
When you put it in your mouth
It separates slowly.

I love the taste of . . .
Lovely crispy chips
With creamy ketchup on
In your mouth they are lovely and crispy.

I hate the taste of . . .
Hot, spicy, smelly curry with naan bread
In your mouth it burns like fire.

Danielle Patterson (10)
Leighton Primary School

Literacy

I am a subject where writing is the key.
Thesauruses are used for better words.
Dictionaries are used for correct spellings.
We are always reminded - nouns, verbs and adjectives.
We use punctuation.
Neat handwriting so the audience can read it.
Pens, pencils, books and rulers are used.
What is the subject?

Dylan Wilson (9)
Leighton Primary School

If . . .

(Based on 'If' by Rudyard Kipling)

If I can succeed and take my course, without leading to split ends
If I can get my products for the first time round
If I can brush through class like the wind in my hair
If I can wash in reality and wash out dreams
If I can do a hairstyle without people looking upset
If I can rely on my talent and not what people say
If I can massage in style and not into dry and damaged
If I can comb through customers without one being disappointed
If I can wash their head of old fashions and bring in a mile of beauty
Then I will be the best stylist ever!

Samantha Cartledge (10)
Leighton Primary School

School Life

I have twelve rooms numbered 1 to 12,
Surrounded by a tall, green fence keeping us safe,
Different sizes of playgrounds for different ages,
Corridors so busy when children charge in and out for lessons,
Many children in assemblies,
Blue, grey and white are our colours,
Head teacher signing, secretaries typing,
Taps running, toilet flushing,
What am I?

Michaela Peacock (10)
Leighton Primary School

Horses Cinquain

Horses
Are tall and strong
Running in a big race
Following the other horses
Grooming.

Rebecca Meech (10)
Leighton Primary School

What We Do At School

I have lots of children in this place,
Lots of room and lots of space.

An office in case someone's ill,
Computers, pens and teacher skill.

Books, trays, tables and toys,
Which get ruined by the boys.

What am I?

Nikki Fletcher (11)
Leighton Primary School

Dinner

Tray collecting
Tasty eating
Table searching
Nikki cooking
Children chatting
Chairs crashing
Drink pouring.

What am I?

Connor Gray (10)
Leighton Primary School

Shoot Out Cinquain

Defoe
West Ham player
Always getting red cards
Hits the ball like a rally car
Football.

Cameron Feguson (10)
Leighton Primary School

Smelly Poem

I hate the smell of . . .
Stinky, sullen cats
With sharp, pointed claws
And mouldy, matted fur.

I love the smell of . . .
Rice cooking in the pan
Sizzling when it gets thrown
Up and down back into the pan.

I hate the smell of . . .
My dad's socks
When he takes them off his feet
The house is stinky.

I love the smell of . . .
Pie cooking in the oven
When it's lovely and hot
When it comes out, yum!

Alarnah Smith (9)
Leighton Primary School

Football Mayhem Cinquain

Great team,
Great, very good,
Skilful, kick ups, free kick,
Christiano Ronaldo scoring,
Helpful.

Luke Brace (9)
Leighton Primary School

Fridge Raider

Watch out for the fridge raider
Loading food into its gob
Chocolate pies and packets of crisps
It really is a slob.

Fat, green and hairy
Wobbly at the knees
The only good thing about him
He eats the mushy peas.

Mince pies and sausage rolls
Chocolate and milkshakes
Baked beans and fries
Creamy buns and fairy cakes.

Remember what I told you
About how the fridge raider comes to tea
So if you get on the wrong side of him
He will eat you and me!

Annie Veenman (10)
Meridian Primary School

The Ocean

The big blue
The giant green.

The ship shaker
The boat breaker.

The fish farm
The squid squirm.

The occy lair
The rocky scare.

Hannah Chandler (11)
Meridian Primary School

Hate And Love

Hate is a lemon
Too sharp, too sweet
The hate soars through your brain all day
And runs through your body
Stays forever

But

Love is a strawberry
Shaped like a heart
Fragile and soft
Once you've bitten into it
The taste stays in your mouth
Always.

Natasha Leigh-Wootton (11)
Meridian Primary School

Ghost

You'd better believe me when I say
That I've seen a *ghost!*
It was big and see-through
It was smooth and weird
It flew around like a bird in the sky
It told me that it'd brought friends
Then the zombie walked in
He just walked around doing nothing
His eyes bobbing around in the air
They freaked me out
They go bump in the night
They haunt you day and night!

Frankie Surmon-Böhr (10)
Meridian Primary School

The Ghost

I was sitting in my bed
Late in my room one night
When a ghost popped by my window
And gave me a big fright.

I jumped up with a startle
With fear and bemuse
When it said, 'Oh, don't worry
My diet's only shoes.'

When I told my parents
They said, 'Don't be silly'
But I know there was a ghost
For my shoes are no longer
Frilly!

Charlotte Hallworth (11)
Meridian Primary School

The Pencil Case

My pencil case is vicious!
I think it's very ambitious,
With its zip, more like jagged teeth,
It wants to eat my friend, Keith!
So please help me, anyone,
Until the job is done,
Quick, before it eats me,
Now for a cup of tea!

Jacob Morris (11)
Meridian Primary School

Jealousy

Jealousy is a kumquat,
Covered by its hard skin,
But on the inside it's sour,
Its juice stings,
Even the sweetest person.

Jealousy is a cherry stone,
Strong and unbreakable,
It is small and difficult to find,
For it is hidden deep down.

Jealousy is a bullet,
It hits so hard,
It is too quick to stop.

Phoebe Sharratt (11)
Meridian Primary School

Right Now Cinquain

Right now
Out of the dark
A three-headed monster
Without warning ate me all up.
I am gone!

Holly Sheppard (10)
Meridian Primary School

The Maths Lesson Haiku

In a maths lesson
Numbers whirling round my head
Where's the answer? Stuck.

Annie Gregory (10)
Meridian Primary School

Loneliness

Loneliness is a grape,
It rolls off by itself
And feels small, small small.
It breaks and all the fluid runs out
And falls into a puddle
And the tiny little seed inside
Cracks, cracks, cracks.
Loneliness is an abandoned island
It's surrounded by noise and movement
And shrinks every day!

Charlotte Horne (11)
Meridian Primary School

Jealousy

Jealousy is a pomegranate,
It has sharp seeds inside
Concealed in a sweet coating
From prying eyes
But when you take a bite from it
Its disguise falls off and the tang
Hits you like a poisoned fang.

Helen Spence-Jones (10)
Meridian Primary School

Springtime Cinquain

Flowers
Lambs are jumping
Birds are singing a song
Trees are dancing with bright green leaves
Sunshine.

Stephanie Cousins (11)
Meridian Primary School

Beautiful Seasons

Flowers in spring
New buds appear
Soon bursting into bloom
When the daisies come
It cuts out the gloom
Pick all that you can
To make the daisy chains long.

Flowers in summer
The sunshine shines
As bright as it can
The poppies come
And the dandelion
The roses come too
To look for you.

Flowers in winter
Holly comes very quick
And the blackthorns in your garden
Although it's cold and icy
Everyone has lots of fun
Little snowdrops appear
Some far away and some near.

Zoe Bishop (9)
Meridian Primary School

Elephants Haiku

Elephants are big
Elephants have big, long trunks
They are big grey lumps!

Alex Sinclair (11)
Meridian Primary School

My Golden Retriever

Even though she's smelly
And she has a big belly,
I love her just the same,
Especially when she's tame.
But even though she's lazy,
When she goes on walks she goes crazy.
But I'll always love her,
Even is she loses all her fur.
I love her!

Alyssa Smith (9)
Meridian Primary School

Stars

Twinkling, tingling in the sky,
Some shoot by,
Biggest, bright up so high,
Some shoot by,
Lazy, light I wonder why?
Some shoot by,
Some shoot by.

Abbie Peek (8)
Meridian Primary School

Shadows Cinquain

Listen
People's voices
Ghosts whispering softly
The gentle footsteps on the snow
Shadows.

Daisy Frame (10)
Meridian Primary School

Caves

The gloomy labyrinth,
The eerie, twisted rock,
The passage in the underground,
Look at that rock,
It's slippery and slimy,
It's freakish and all shiny,
Look at those walls,
Those jagged, dripping walls,
They're wet and all mirey,
I bet they're really grimy.

Elizabeth Turland (8)
Meridian Primary School

The Weather Forecast Cinquain

Weather,
Ridiculous,
Twelve noon during the day,
A pigeon scuttled in a tree,
Freezing.

Hannah Albone (10)
Meridian Primary School

Warning For Cheese Lovers Haiku

There's no need for cheese
Full of holes and mouldy bits
Ban cheese forever!

Sarah Mallinson (11)
Meridian Primary School

Snails

Snails are slimy,
Snails are strong,
Snails can carry
Their shells on
Their backs.

Snails are small,
Snails are sliding,
Snails can carry
Their shells on
Their backs.

Snails are slippy,
Snails are smooth,
Snails can carry
Their shells on
Their backs.

Emily Jameson (9)
Meridian Primary School

My Broken Heart

My heart is cold, my heart is sad
I'm feeling tired, I'm feeling bad

I sit here sad and really lonely
My heart is breaking very slowly

No matter what I've already done
I hope I'll be your number one

I need to see if we can start
To mend the pieces of my broken heart.

Aliénor Longson (9)
Meridian Primary School

My Family

My mum is always lazy
You might say she's crazy.

Funky sister's always mad
And her singing's very bad.

My dad is always rushing
I can understand why he's always crashing.

Little sister always wails
You might think she's in jail!

I don't understand why Polly parrot squeaks
Sunny cat always stalks.

Friendly brother, Tom, is always efficient
Ungrateful brother, Alex, is always disobedient.

Nanny always looks after us
New adventures on the bus.

You might say it's always sunny
Why is my family so funny?

Chloë Bidwell (9)
Meridian Primary School

Grandad

G reat is my grandad
R eally funny too!
A lways makes me laugh
N utty is his name
D readful are his jokes!
A ngry he is never
D edicated to his family always.

Liam Sutton (9)
Meridian Primary School

The Volcano

Deep down beneath the Earth's crust,
The gases swivelling and turning around,
Whooossshhh!
The lava's ready to emerge from its bed,
Crackling and bubbling beneath the Earth's crust.
No one can hear it coming yet,
It's as quiet as a mouse.

The world's in danger of a breathtaking volcano,
The lava's crawling up it,
Deadly things are going to happen.
Silence across the world.
Only that one thing - silence.
It starts to rumble.
An earthquake crushes a house,
Two houses, then three.

Do the people suspect it, or are they blind?
For the volcanoes are coming . . .
Coming . . . coming.
Smoke slowly creeps out until *crash!*
Angry smoke melting everything in its way.
Ash and rock swim in the smoke
And are faster than a bullet from a gun.

Now the lava takes its turn, deadlier than ever.
Melting, bubbling, squashing,
It trickles down the side of the volcano,
Down to towns, down to forests
And down to the people.

A bare, cold, scary place, a town is after an eruption.
No trees, no houses, no life.
No one having fun, no one shouting and playing,
No one, not anything.

Now the people start to come back
To see the trees that start to grow,
To live their lives,
To forget about it all.
Meanwhile, the volcano sleeps for hundreds of years,
Until the next
Eruption!

Linda Campo (10)
Middlefield Community Primary School

The Volcano's Life

Deep beneath the Earth's crust,
In the mantle,
A pressure is building,
Waiting to burst out and ooze to the ground,
Destroying anything in its path.
It begins to bubble, sizzle
And becomes so hot,
It will burst out at any moment.
It is ready to burst out at any time.

Rumble, rumble, the ground starts shaking,
Rocks and boulders are falling,
It feels like the ground is falling apart.
The volcano is swelling.
Then nothing.
Everything stops.
Nothing moves.
The magma chamber is like a heart
Still pumping lava beneath the Earth.
The people rebuild their home and move back.
It is over.
The terror of the volcano is over . . .
For now.

Gregory Mason (10)
Middlefield Community Primary School

A Volcano

Under the Earth's crust, pressure is building up.
The molten liquid rock is bubbling, crackling and sizzling.
It's waiting to burst out.
The gases are making more molten rock.
It's waiting to sizzle.
It's waiting to come out and be free.

The volcano is swelling.
There are small, rumbling earthquakes.
Earthquakes shattering, telling something.
They are warning about a terrible thing about to happen.
An eruption is coming.
But it's all gone calm.
Nothing, no earthquakes to warn, no swelling volcano.

Suddenly a pyroclastic flow.
Thundering, riding down the road of death.
It's coming fast, quick,
Thundering down like an avalanche.
Extremely hot ash and gas moving to the village.
Crunch, smash, things explode, but you can't see them.

Bang! Lava flies into the air.
The lava is starting to flow
Like fire going down the volcano.
Slide! Sometimes fast, sometimes slow
And then it sets into rock, nothing but rock.

The village is destroyed.
Towns and countryside are ruined.
Some people escaped just in time.
They did not want to leave their homes.
They did though.
Not many people managed,
But they had to.

People come back, the volcano's asleep.
They also came back for the land fertilized by the volcano.
The people put it to the back of their minds.
The towns and villages are built back,
But one day, in another year or decade perhaps,
Deep beneath the Earth's crust . . .

Jacob Dawson (10)
Middlefield Community Primary School

What Am I?

I am like the top of an ice cream,
Trickling down the cone's edge.

I am like milk,
Spilt on the table.

I am like flour,
Being sieved to bake a cake.

I am like whipped cream,
Being squeezed on a cake.

I am like a pillow,
When it is freshly made on your bed.

I am like a gravel path,
When you stamp on it.

I am like white pieces of paper,
Floating onto the ground.

What am I?

Mark Dawson (9)
Middlefield Community Primary School

The Volcano

Deep beneath the Earth's crust,
There is a pressure building - baking.
Molten rock is boiling under the Earth,
Sizzling, crackling.
The gas is building up to make the volcano erupt.
The gas has moved.

Then rumbling under the ground,
Cracking, crumbling.
People screaming, shouting,
Not very big, but still rumbling.
Now all is silence.
No screaming, no shouting,
Just silence!

Then suddenly, the evil pyroclastic flow,
Boiling, baking.
Travelling so fast,
Like an avalanche of snow,
So hot, if anything touched it,
It would melt.
It's getting ready to deal its final card.
Neatly, quickly.

Kaboom!
The volcano exploding, erupting.
The lava oozes and trickles into the village,
Oozing, trickling.
It's just like a red fire,
Burning, boiling,
A river of molten rock.

After, all is silence.
Nothing moves, no noise.
No nothing.
The lava has cooled,
It has become rock.

The volcano is sleeping,
Until it decides to erupt again.

Harrison Smith (10)
Middlefield Community Primary School

Volcano

Deep down low,
Beyond the Earth's crust
A pressure builds up
That could knock
A stampede of elephants down.
The molten liquid rock
Crackles and bubbles as it
Is desperate to burst out.

Rumble, rumble, the ground is moving.
The volcano swells like a sponge cake in an oven.
Then silence, nothing moves, no sound,
It's getting ready to blow.

Suddenly, a hiss fills the air,
A pyroclastic flow
Moves as fast as an avalanche.
It destroys everything in its path,
Everyone knows to move.

Bang!
An explosion fills the air,
Lava is flowing
Down the side of the volcano
Like a river flowing
Through the rocks.

After the bang,
There is nothing around.
Everything destroyed, gone.
The houses are crushed
Like a giant has stamped on them.
Friends, family, buried.

Sshh!
The volcano goes back to sleep.
Lava is settling.
Getting ready below
For another explosion
In thousands of years to come.

Lorna Childs (11)
Middlefield Community Primary School

The Volcano!

Deep down beneath the Earth's crust,
Power and pressure is building up.
It could kill forty armies of men.
The magma chamber is gurgling and bubbling,
Waiting to pour out and trickle down.
Gases are waiting to fill the air.

Rumble! Rumble!
Warning signs are standing still,
Not moving, not at all.
Small earthquakes,
Rumbling, shaking!
The volcano starts to swell.
There's a silence,
A deadly silence.

The volcano starts to crack.
Out comes the blistering pyroclastic flow.
It will destroy anything in its path,
Travelling very, very fast,
Like an avalanche.

Suddenly *bang!*
The volcano has erupted.
It is like thunder, but deadlier.
Like a fizzy drink being opened after it's been shaken up.
But worse!
The town's people stop and stare.

After a while,
There's lava and molten rock
Trickling and oozing down,
Like a river flowing fast.
It moves as fast as a tornado,
A bad tornado!

Some people from the town try to escape,
Others think there's no point.
Some just lie there.
After a while it sets,
Like cement.
All is quiet,
Nothing but silence.

After a while, people that survived
Started to look through all the rubble.
They started to build the town again
And push it to the back of their minds.
The volcano sleeps,
But it is still going on beneath the Earth's crust.

Rebecca Willard (10)
Middlefield Community Primary School

The Bakery

I am outside looking inside
At all the lovely cakes.
Bakery doors ringing,
Taste buds tingling,
Microwaves dinging,
Wishing the cake was mine.
So I go in
And buy my chocolate cream cake,
But when it's all gone,
I really want more,
So I search in my pockets
To try and find money,
But I've already spent it
On my lovely chocolate cream cake.
I am inside wishing to buy my cake.

Lincoln Miles (10)
Middlefield Community Primary School

Eruption!

Deep beneath the Earth's crust,
Where men would be crushed,
A chamber is building,
Building up pressure
Able to crush boulders.
Molten rock is boiling,
Fizzing, waking,
Readying itself
To burst and destroy,
Readying itself to kill.

Rumble, rumble!
The earthquake comes -
The first of many warnings.
The volcano, it grows,
It expands and cracks.
Readying itself to kill.
Then . . . silence.
A deathly silence.
Nothing moves or breathes,
Nothing.
There is silence.

The volcano, it explodes!
But no ash and sparks
Escape its jaws.
A gas, a deadly gas
Comes pelting down
Like a bullet from a gun,
But travelling much faster.

Whoosh! Hiss!
The gas makes sounds,
Horrid sounds that scare.
The gas is hot, blisteringly hot,
Hot enough to kill.
The deadly avalanche,
It engulfs everything,
The last warning before
The final eruption.

And now, what everyone has dreaded
Comes true. It explodes!
A huge cloud of ash
And sparks come forth
From the dark jaws of death
And a deadly river
Of molten rock comes
Speeding down the valleyside.

People scream and run.
Where to run? Nowhere!
But some escape before
The eruption, during the warning signs.
Others are not so lucky.
Screams of death pierce the night air,
Screams that pierce the sky.

Then it's over, after days,
Months even, it's over.
People forget, they come back
To what used to be home.
They rebuild, restock supplies,
Until the next . . .
Eruption!

Douglas Shillito (11)
Middlefield Community Primary School

Not A Test!

I am inside looking outside,
I am trapped in a cage,
A living creature, not a test.
I feel the sting of the needle,
Animal friends howling and crying,
A man leaning over my cage,
It's my turn next.
I am inside looking outside.

James Poulton (10)
Middlefield Community Primary School

Volcano

Deep beneath the Earth's crust
A pressure builds up
Which could turn a submarine
Into a sardine can.
The gases bubble
Like soapsuds in water
The magma waiting to burst out
Like a newborn chick in an egg
To destroy anything in its path
Of hot, boiling gas.

The warning signs come now
Boom! An earthquake cracks open the earth
Like the opening of a packet of crisps, ferociously
The volcano swells and then
A deadly silence.

Suddenly, a pryroclastic flow erupts
And a blistering, poker-hot ash avalanche
Comes thundering down
Like ten sports cars at full speed
Filled with nitro in the engine
It destroys everything in its path
Like a madman with a chainsaw.

Bang!
An explosion worse than the A-bomb
Hits the ground
Lava and magma pour and spout out
Like a running tap
It is hotter than an oven on full heat.

Argh!
The people scream and run
Like headless chickens
Whilst the buildings tumble down
Like building blocks
And a hurry of people run away
But the engine of the volcano
Is too fast for them.

A smell of death is in the air
Then the engine splutters
Stops
A deadly silence follows
The volcano sleeps, slowly adrift
The victims frozen in ash.

Jethro Steel (11)
Middlefield Community Primary School

The Abandoned Cat

I am inside, looking outside
Wishing to be free
Miserable and abandoned
Lonely and annoyed
Seeing other cats playing
Chasing around birds
Wishing I could too
But trapped in a shed
I am feeling scared and depressed
Cats making fun of me outside
Laughing, joking
Sticking tongues out at me
Wishing to be free
I am inside, looking outside.

Samantha Mitchell (11)
Middlefield Community Primary School

The Eruption

Deep, deep under the Earth's crust
There is a force waking up
That could destroy almost anything
The liquid molten rock crackles
Sizzles and bubbles
Ready to burst out
The gases hissing as it moves.

Crack, crack
The volcano swells, getting bigger
Like a bee sting
The first of the warning signs
Rumble, rumble, small earthquakes
Like an upset tummy
But then
Nothing!

Suddenly
Boom, boom
Like a charging bull
Flying high as birds
Whoosh, going faster than racing cars
Destroying anything
The boiling gas and rock
Blisters
And wipes out man and anything else.

Bang, boom
Lava flows down the
Volcano
Toasting forests like bread
Knocking down buildings
Getting slower until
It stops.

Families flee before
The lava catches them
Many are killed
Others are lucky
Now silence
The volcano sleeps
Sitting dormant
All its victims around it
Death
Silence.

Luke Thomas (10)
Middlefield Community Primary School

What Am I?

I am like a giant cookie flying
with the chocolate chips.

I am a streetlight flashing on and off
like lightning.

I am a half-eaten Jaffa cake
in the dark-blue sky.

I'm a ghostly, white ball
bouncing through the sky.

I'm a bright streetlight to Heaven.
I'm a giant pearl glistening in the sky.

What am I?

Abagail Rothwell (10)
Middlefield Community Primary School

The Horse That Was Scared

I am inside looking outside,
Misty scenes are moving in closer,
The wind brings frightening footsteps,
My hooves are rustling the hay,
The barn doors are squeaking,
I hear wolves howling and owls hooting,
My eyes are darting around to see,
My eyes widen with horror,
I am inside looking outside.

Thomas Warne (11)
Middlefield Community Primary School

Guilty In The Cell

I am inside looking outside,
Listening to people having fun outside.
The cell smells like rotten eggs,
I can't stand it anymore.
Feeling guilty for what I have done,
Freezing cold in my cell at night.
Wishing to be free,
I am inside looking outside.

Samuel Page (9)
Middlefield Community Primary School

What Am I?

I am like a mum cleaning a room,
Using a vacuum cleaner, sucking up dust.

I am like a bulldozer smashing houses down,
Day in, day out.

I am like a crocodile
Chewing up houses.

What am I?

Jonathan Fromant (9)
Middlefield Community Primary School

I Want To Be Free

I am inside, looking outside
Out the glass windows, wishing to be free
Seeing all the snow and people being free
And I am really wanting to get out of here
Inside you can hear toys and people arguing
I am grounded and alone
I am furious, mad and unhappy
Please let me out
Looking out the glass windows, wishing to be free
I am inside, looking outside,
Please let me be free.

Daniel Birkinshaw (11)
Middlefield Community Primary School

The Restaurant

I am staring out the restaurant windows,
Waiting for my meal,
Seeing waiters walking slowly by.
People eating
Bangers and mash,
Wishing it was mine.
I'm starting to feel jealous,
Grumpy and frustrated,
Hungry and cross.
Wishing to be fed,
I am inside, looking out.

Jamie McDonald (10)
Middlefield Community Primary School

Can't Get Out

I am inside, squinting outside of the dog cage.
The bitter cold wind swipes,
The freezing car rumbles,
My eyes fill with horror.
It is getting misty and murky,
I see the farmer's furious face
And I hear the creaking trees surrounding me,
The rustling of the boxes,
The bitter cold wind swipes,
I am inside squinting outside,
But I am abandoned.

Ryan Gore (10)
Middlefield Community Primary School

The Wish Dog

I am inside looking outside.
The feeling of being behind bars makes me whimper.
Worried people won't take me home.
Watching people walk past.
Freezing cold every night.
Sniffing the cold air that freezes me.
Wishing to be free.
I am inside looking outside.

Cory Houghton (9)
Middlefield Community Primary School

Trapped Inside

I am inside, listening outside
Listening to the roaring sea,
The cracking trees which enter my dreams
And turn them into nightmares,
Crashing hailstones against the wall,
The clapping thunder,
Wanting to wake my mum,
Howling winds driving me further under my duvet,
The dustbins tumbling over
And creaking windows.
I am inside, listening outside.

Aiden Clarke (11)
Middlefield Community Primary School

Inside Looking Out

I am inside my burrow, but peeking out
I can't see the peaceful green grass
But I can see large yellow robots
My friends are getting killed by the tracks they make
I am inside my burrow
Looking out at a big, black road
They say it's the future
It's not mine
I am inside, peeking out
I'm frightened of change.

Ryan Pearce (11)
Middlefield Community Primary School

What Am I?

I am like a thousand tears,
dripping down your face on a winter's day.

I am like a shower,
sprinkling down your back.

I am like a sprinkler
in your garden.

I am like sparrows
on your roof.

I am like a car
on gravel.

What am I?

Brady Mayes (10)
Middlefield Community Primary School

My Friends Are Late

I am inside looking outside,
Wishing to be free.
I'm waiting for my friends to knock,
But the clock is broken.
Everybody who I invited is a bit late,
For the meal is getting cold.
I am inside looking outside.

Jordan Reynolds (9)
Middlefield Community Primary School

Hedgehog

I am inside looking outside
The leaves on my furry face
Wondering, wishing, hoping
That the gunshots will soon stop
In my hedgerow worried to leave
Worried, annoyed, scared
I wish I was with my family still
I am by myself, ready to protect
But inside I am anxious,
Desperately alone.
I am inside looking outside.

Benjamin Miles (10)
Middlefield Community Primary School

Vets

I am inside, looking out
Waiting to hear good news.
I sit frozen on the spot
Cats cry and dogs whimper.
Was it because of me
My dog is here?
Worried faces surround me
I feel lonely and heartbroken.
Time paces as if hours have gone
Vets come and pace, trying to cheer people up.
I am inside, looking out.

Hannah Cooley (10)
Middlefield Community Primary School

What Am I?

I am like a football
being kicked up in the air.
I am like a lemon in the sky
being squashed flat.
I am like a pancake
with butter being spread on it.
I am like a clock
telling you the time.

What am I?

Liam Hill (10)
Middlefield Community Primary School

The Sea

The sea
Slowly
Stalking the beach
Then
It lashes out
Striking
The force of an elephant
Crashes
Slam
Into the rock
Then
Nothing, the rock has gone
And
Silence, once more.

Oscar O'Brien (10)
Parnwell Primary School

Owl

Awakes
Hungrily glares
Swiftly, silently swoops
At any prey
He dares
Circling high
In the big, black sky
One shall die . . .
Owl makes his
Choice
A loud screech in his
Voice
Reach the ground
For a little mouse
An enjoyable
Feast
Happy and content
Owl is fed
Snuggles down tight
Ready for the
Next night . . .

Sophia Lane (11)
Parnwell Primary School

Countryside

Feel the fresh air in the sky,
People playing in the fields,
Birds are black,
Sun hovering in the sky,
Trees are rustling like tissue paper,
Warm weather,
Lovely breeze drifting by,
All is calm, all is restful.

Katie Evans (11)
Parnwell Primary School

Owl

Flying like the wind
Swooping down to kill its
Prey,
Silence, silence,
Who-whooing in the night,
Getting into a fight.
Eyes like amber,
Looking all around.
Gripping its death
And eating its prey.
Dark through the night,
Owl . . .
Was . . .
Is . . .

Scott Neil (10)
Parnwell Primary School

Owl

Swooping through the night,
Flying,
Watching,
Catching its prey,
Burning, amber, sight,
Who-whooing,
Sitting,
Standing,
Into the silence it goes,
Gripping what it sees,
Its feathers as soft as a pillow,
Its eyes as big as headlights,
Who? Who? Who?

Katie Andresen (11)
Parnwell Primary School

T-Rex

It wants to show its fierce appearance
From the past of the start
It spreads its disease
Of death
The fur no longer seems soft
When the trees shiver with fear
It opens its mouth to find a sweet taste
It waits
Until the time is right
It hides
Over the cloud
Oh, do not move
It might be behind you
Its big teeth
It's huge
It's terrifying
Run! Hide!
More fun for it
It's waiting and waiting
It will devastate you
If you touch its coat, round its neck
Its claws are as sharp
As its hearing and sight
It waits until next time.

Aidan Bates (10)
Parnwell Primary School

Owl

Owl . . .
Gliding through the night
His laser beam eyes
He sights prey
He swoops down
Strike one
He misses
Strike two
He misses again
Strike three
Again he misses
He gains his confidence
Lightning strike
He hits
His claws
Sinking into its skin like daggers
Silently
Silently . . .

Peter Denton (11)
Parnwell Primary School

Owl

Swooping low,
Through the skies,
Rustling feathers,
Amber eyes.
Coming out,
To catch its prey,
Alive by night,
Dead by day.
Its deadly screech,
Its tu-whit tu-whoo,
Its deafening howl,
Its whoo-whoo-whoo.

Emma Smith (11)
Parnwell Primary School

Owl

Whose feathers spread
Out in the sky
Under a tree
Just past
Nigh
Complete silence
Then . . .
A small, young mouse scuttles
Out of its den
Every movement
Every sound
The owl
Instantly
Will let it be found.

Jasmine Joyce (11)
Parnwell Primary School

The Sea

Splashy waves splashing on rocks
Clawing and pawing the sand like a fox.
The sea is tough
Just like a tidal wave that's rough.
People screaming
With the sea gleaming.

Splashy waves splashing on rocks
Clashing and bashing against the docks.
Playing with streams and dancing with ditches
Flying like fairies and rushing like witches.
The waves swirling
And the water curling.

Joel Gomes (10)
Parnwell Primary School

If I Had Wings

If I had wings
I would touch the beautiful birds
That swoop past me.

If I had wings
I would gaze at the dark blue
Sea and oceans that sparkle
In the sun.

If I had wings
I would taste the colours
Of the rainbow
That glisten in the sun.

If I had wings
I would smell the scent of roses
That cling like a magnet
To the ground.

If I had wings
I would listen to the raindrops
That splash down out of the
Clouds.

If I had wings
I would dream of the tropical
Rainforests and surfing
On the seas.

Christopher Bates
Priory Junior School

If I Had Wings

If I had wings
I would taste the candy cotton clouds
As I glide between them.

If I had wings
I would listen to the sound of the wind howling
As I glide up to space.

If I had wings
I would smell the perfume of the roses
As I float among them.

If I had wings
I would perch on the tops of trees
And reach up to the clouds above me.

If I had wings
I would gaze at the mountains below
As I make my way back down the Earth.

Jamie Butler (10)
Priory Junior School

If I Had Wings

If I had wings
I would touch the flowers
and touch the trees.

If I had wings
I would stroke
a cat that is softer
than a cloud.

If I had wings
I would dream away my days.

Jessica Miller (9)
Priory Junior School

If I Had Wings

If I had wings,
I would finger the white fluffy clouds,
As I'd glide through the fresh air,
With the sun rising behind me.

If I had wings,
I would graze on a growing apple,
Comfortably sat on the top
Of a green tree.

If I had wings,
I would listen to the seagulls,
Flying round and round over the
Clear blue sea.

If I had wings,
I would inhale the beautiful
Scent of the red roses floating
In the breeze.

If I had wings,
I would spy on a parrot,
Perched on a branch in a tropical
Rainforest.

If I had wings,
I would dream of the fantastic
Sunset as it shines down on
The clear blue glittering sea.

Faith Hewitt (10)
Priory Junior School

If I Had Wings

If I had wings
I would touch the little leaves as they
rustle in the wind.

If I had wings
I would taste the stars as they
twinkle in my teeth.

If I had wings
I would sniff the salty seawater on
the beautiful sunny beach.

If I had wings
I would gaze at the sun shining all
day long.

If I had wings
I would listen to the sound of the
seagulls gliding around the sky.

If I had wings
I would dream of flying over the traffic
as the cars move and stop.

Daniel Biddle (9)
Priory Junior School

Richard Bites The Dust

In 1485 the Battle of Bosworth began,
It started with a big clang.
Cannons were here, cannons were there, cannons were everywhere.
Lots of people died and relatives cried,
People are watching the news while the people
are given clues.

Jade Ursell & Josh Woodend (9)
Priory Junior School

If I Had Wings

If I had wings,
I would spot the fish swimming
and relaxing in the deep blue sea.

If I had wings,
I would eat pieces of the sun
as hot as chilli sauce.

If I had wings,
I would take in the wonderful
sound of beautiful wildlife.

If I had wings,
I would take a deep breath
of lovely fresh air.

If I had wings,
I would peek over the highest mountain
taking my breath right away.

If I had wings,
I would see a whole new world
of calming peace and quiet.

Adam Williams (10)
Priory Junior School

The Bosworth Battle

The battle began for the fight was to come,
There were smashes and bashes,
Lord Stanley gave men to help Henry be king,
They fought like doghogs and rats and bats and cats.

Richard got knocked off his horse and all the men went galore,
Richard got stabbed, all the men were killing him bad,
They found the crown in a thorn bush, the thistles and bristles,
Henry got crowned and the war was over.

Liam Brook (9)
Priory Junior School

The Bosworth War

The war for the king,
The war for the just,
The war for the truth,
The war for the courage,
The brave strong soldier,
The fear in the eye,
The fight for the men,
The bashing and the crashing,
The fight for mankind,
The battle of the royal,
The battle for the leadership,
The battle for the crown,
The crown in the thorns,
The stabbing and the smashing,
Henry wears the crown
The end of the war,
The whistle in the wind as the brave soldiers leave.

Nicole Searle (10)
Priory Junior School

In A Deserted Creepy Castle

A boy called Jim walked up the hill,
And found a deserted castle.
He walked right in and there in front of him,
Was a spooky ghost!

Out of the walls came all the ghost's friends,
And scared him out of his skin.
Along came the horseman,
The boy raised his saucepan and knocked him
Off his horse!

The boy had had enough
He ran out with his stuff
Pegged it down the hill and met his mother Jill.

Thomas Bryon (9) & Alastair Guinee (10)
Priory Junior School

If I Had Wings

If I had wings,
I would reach up and feel the moon,
and stay up there with its gloomy light.

If I had wings,
I would taste a piece of the flowing clouds
with the scent of cream.

If I had wings,
I would listen to the brilliant
songs from the birds like musical instruments.

If I had wings,
I would breathe in the airy breeze
Just like paradise.

If I had wings,
I would stare at the things
trapped down below, like seeing little dolls
running around.

Heather Linnell (10)
Priory Junior School

If I Had Wings

If I had wings I would fly to Neptune
and drink its fluids.

If I had wings I would fly to a rainforest
and touch the sloth moving slowly.

If I had wings I would hear an aeroplane
zoom past me.

If I had wings I would see the cool view of
America's lovely sun.

If I had wings I would smell the boiling
volcano's breath.

Jack Bramley (9)
Priory Junior School

If I Had Wings

If I had wings I would
rub the ruins
of the Grand Canyon.

If I had wings I would
gaze at the moonlight
sky like a space robot.

If I had wings I would
munch the crust
of a hot volcano.

If I had wings I would
listen to the sea crashing
against the mountain.

If I had wings I would
inhale the grassy rocky
mountain.

If I had wings I would
dream that I could fly
anywhere in the world.

Jordan Adams (9)
Priory Junior School

The Deserted Castle

On the highest mountain on the southest south
Was an old deserted castle long forgotten.
Icy halls cold and dusty,
Shivery passages and really haunted,
Dungeons disgusting and full of horrid skeletons,
Long ago a fierce battle ended in a ferocious fire,
Everyone perished in the horrible fire,
Long forgotten.

Charlie Jordan (9)
Priory Junior School

Castle Of Doom

As we walked in we heard the
floorboard creak,
and peered out of the dusty window
it was terribly steep.

We looked around at the jewellery
and crown
and the floor was covered in horrible
brown.

We saw a ghost coming towards us
it seemed to be in a terrible fuss.

And we went into the dining room
we saw some plates and jars and
a silver shining spoon.

We ran out of the door in a terrible scream.
It seemed to be like a dream.

Jade Barnes (10)
Priory Junior School

The Deserted Castle

On the highest mountain
Was a deserted castle
In the southest south,
Long forgotten, long forgotten,
Icy halls all cold and dusty.
Shivery passages sooty and haunted,
Scary graves filled with gold and bones,
Dungeons disgusting and full of wacky skeletons,
Long forgotten, long forgotten,
Long ago a fierce battle ended in a ferocious fire,
Long forgotten, long forgotten.

Wesley Upton (9)
Priory Junior School

The Castle Of Shadows

In a dark, dark castle
There was a shadow ghoul
Any man who entered
Was a big, big fool!

But there was a man who entered
Who was a big brave knight
But he didn't know
He was in for a fright, fright, fright!

The knight went to bed
Being rather still
Once he was woken up
He was very, very ill!

There was a dark, dark castle
Where a shadow ghoul lived
Any man who entered
Was a big, big fool!

Kurt Sanders (9)
Priory Junior School

The Sunken Ship

There was, long ago, a ship,
Which sailed in the Atlantic Ocean
It went into battle and was hit by a ship
Lost in the sea, all dignity forgotten
Now it's a sunken ship
With all crew lost.

It is now just a wreck,
On the ocean floor
Nothing but planks
And a couple of sails.

Thomas Dinsdale (9)
Priory Junior School

If I Had Wings

If I had wings,
I would lick a mouthwatering ice cream on a scorching day.

If I had wings,
I would taste the summer fruits from evergreen trees.

If I had wings,
I would touch the raindrops and feel them falling down quickly
onto the ground.

If I had wings,
I would smell the wetness of the ground and hear the stomp
of my feet.

If I had wings,
I would fly slowly over a tropical Amazon forest and hear all the
noises of the creatures.

If I had wings,
I would fly carefully over Angel Falls and taste the water.

If I had wings,
I would see the beautiful countryside and hear the soft breeze.

If I had wings,
I would fly swiftly to the beach and feel the rippling waves on the
soft yellow sand.

If I had wings,
I would see Egyptian tombs and poisonous traps waiting to kill.

Shanice Muir (10)
Priory Junior School

The Haunted Castle

There was an abandoned old castle,
Filled with lots of ghosts,
Skeletons and ghouls,
But dead bodies followed you the most.

Skeletons mastered the portcullis,
Ghouls looked after the drawbridge with care,
Everywhere they went,
There was something there.

In the dungeon there was a dragon,
Who guarded the door,
Outside the door there was a ghost,
Who waited by the floor.

So if you ever see this castle
Don't go anywhere near,
For if you do,
You will encounter lots of fear.

Charlotte Goodwin & Thomas Hale (10)
Priory Junior School

The Battle Of Bosworth

The Battle of Bosworth came
King Richard thought he would win
No one was carrying a flame
Some people came to kill him.

They found a crown
In a thorn bush
When Henry saw the crown
He shouted, 'Come on down.'

All the people bowed to his feet,
Henry was the new king.
They all deserved a special treat
Then they were all proud.

Chelsey Mills (9)
Priory Junior School

The Ghost And The Castle!

Walk through the creaking doors,
Go through the dusty hall,
Walk up the stinky, smelly,
Dusty, dirty stairs.

There was a scream, a terrible scream,
In the dark, dark, spooky, spooky room,
There was a scream.

I went into the room,
There was no one to be seen.
I saw a shadow
On the wall.

I did scream, I know I did,
Then there was a repeated scream.
I ran away from the spooky, spooky, castle.

Emma Storey (9)
Priory Junior School

The Battle Of Bosworth

It all happened in 1486
When Richard took on Henry,
The battle only lasted two hours
With Henry attacking first,
Then Richard attacked Henry
Henry with 5,000 men
Then Richard with 10,000.

Richard was knocked off his horse
Then got killed by Henry,
Richard's crown was found under a gorse bush
Then Henry became king.

Joseph Kokotka (10)
Priory Junior School

The Undead Castle

Come in if you dare,
Argh,
If you do you'll have a scare,
Ooo! Ooo!

Armed skeletons come out the wall,
Armour on head to toe,
They are short so stamp on them if you're tall,
They crush easily as they are weak.

Mad axemen in the way,
Dodge their axes to survive,
Be careful as the axes sway,
If you don't you'll be in pieces.

Don't disturb the undead's castle again,
Ooo! Ooo!
If you do, you'll receive a lot of pain,
Argh!

Nathan Austin & Alastair Edwards (9)
Priory Junior School

If I Had Wings

If I had wings,
I would fly to Australia
And race with the kangaroos.

If I had wings,
I would swim with the fish
In the ocean blue.

If I had wings,
I would soar through the universe
And see how big it was.

If I had wings,
I would touch the highest mountains
And sit there all day long.

Michelle Fletcher (10)
Priory Junior School

If I Had Wings

If I had wings
I would sit on a cloud
and see the blackbirds fly by.

If I had wings
I would bite the red-hot sun to see how
it will burn in my mouth.

If I had wings
I would walk on thin air.

If I had wings
I would smell the glowing stars
to see what they smell like.

If I had wings
I would touch the planets to see
what they feel like.

Laura Teale (9)
Priory Junior School

If I Had Wings

If I had wings,
I would glide over the mountains
And feel the breeze.

If I had wings,
I would glide the rainbow
And splash colours everywhere.

If I had wings,
I would look down below
And see a wonderful view.

If I had wings,
I would listen to the aeroplanes,
And jets zooming past.

James Wakefield (9)
Priory Junior School

If I Had Wings,

If I had wings,
I would fly into the centre of the Earth
and taste the core.

If I had wings,
I would fly to the top of a big tree
and watch all the people do their things.

If I had wings,
I would fly to the boiling hot sun and
touch the wave of heat that comes from it.

If I had wings,
I would fly to a dark cave and hear
the echo when I talk.

If I had wings,
I would fly to China and smell the
spicy curry that they like.

Jessica James (10)
Priory Junior School

If I Had Wings

If I had wings
I would sprint across the big wet sea
To get to the blue middle.

If I had wings
I would climb mountains
And look at the world below.

If I had wings
I would fly with the planes
And wave at the sleepy passengers.

If I had wings
I would jump into space
And touch Pluto's icy base.

Abbie Miles (9)
Priory Junior School

The Battle Of Bosworth

Richard at the top of the hill
Henry at the bottom,
The battle's just beginning,
But when will the battle end?

Richard has 10,000 men,
Henry only 5,000,
I wonder who will win
And when will the battle end?

Lord Stanley comes to the rescue with 3,000 men,
Richard comes charging down the hill,
When will the battle end?

Henry's men waited at the bottom of the hill.
Richard got surrounded,
And dragged off his horse.
This is when the battle ends.

Henry found the crown in a bush
Henry took the throne
Henry VII is our new king.

Lottie Judge (10)
Priory Junior School

If I Had Wings

If I had wings . . .
I would fly to the top of a tree and look at the
leaves rustling down below.

If I had wings,
I would nibble a piece of the crusty sun as I fall
back down to Earth.

If I had wings,
I would fly to the sky and cuddle a cloud
that feels like cotton wool.

If I had wings,
I would listen to the fire-breathing volcano as it
explodes.

If I had wings,
I would fly to Wonderland and smell the gazy
green grass.

If I had wings,
I would take a rubber up to the sky and
rub out all the bad things in life!

Larissa Crisp (9)
Priory Junior School

If I Had Wings

If I had wings,
I would sit on the moon
and gaze at the shiny stars glisten
in the bright sky.

If I had wings,
I would listen to the strong wind
zoom past me.

If I had wings,
I would fly high in the sky
and watch the bright sun go down at night!

If I had wings,
I would fly to India,
and taste the food they eat.

If I had wings,
I would fly to the top of a colourful rainbow
and smell the crystal clear air.

If I had wings,
I would fly to the top of the bright sky,
and fall asleep on a big fluffy cloud.

Maisie Grant (10)
Priory Junior School

The Battle Of Bosworth

Two armies marched to war,
One to the top of the hill,
Both the armies looking keen,
The leaders almost as mean.

King Richard ordered a charge,
Down the hill men came.
Swords flashed, armour clashed,
Henry's army being bashed,
A violent assault of death.

Archers fire into the mire,
A hundred more are slain.
Richard's army closed in,
Henry's hopes into the bin.

Lord Stanley came in,
A hundred more dead,
The tide started to turn,
While the timber arrows burn,
A valiant assault of death.

Richard mounted his horse,
Rallying up his men's hopes,
Then charged with fury,
Making others look puny,
As he slew on his left and right.

Henry's men jabbed at Richard,
Wounding him savagely.
They pulled him off his horse,
And killed him using brute force.
A valiant assault of death,
Into the Devil's lair!
Into the Devil's lair!

Sam Johnston (10)
Priory Junior School

If I Had Wings

If I had wings,
I would fly round
the solar system
and taste a bit
out of every planet.

If I had wings,
I would go up to Heaven
and have a talk with God.

If I had wings,
I would fly to a big bushy cloud,
and sit there and watch the
world go by.

If I had wings,
I would see the little children play
in the exciting park.

If I had wings,
I would go and taste all the different
food from a different country.

Rosie Ball (10)
Priory Junior School

Dead Man's Grave

In a creepy castle,
I see a monster,
And a half-eaten skeleton.

I hear a noise, I start to run,
My veins are tickling,
Something's begun.

I open a door,
And I shiver,
I fall on the floor,
Because I see a ghost.

I can't get out,
I start to fall,
I hear screaming,
Am going to die.

I am leaving, I will live another day,
I've got to the door, I've fallen,
Am dead!

Richard Curr (10)
Priory Junior School

If I Had Wings

If I had wings,
I would fly to the moon and
gaze down on the Earth's surface.

If I had wings,
I would fly to sniff the scent
of master chefs at work.

If I had wings,
I would fly to feel the furs
of wild animals.

If I had wings,
I would venture to taste
sensational wines.

If I had wings,
I would fly to hear the
roar of truly terrifying beasts.

Luke Gardiner (10)
Priory Junior School

The Sunken Ship

Long, long ago was a pirate ship which sailed the Seven Seas.
The pirate's name was Black Hook Bees.

One day there was a storm which awoke Black Hook Bees
                                                    with a fright.
The storm made it very dark so it looked like night.

A few hours later the boat had sunk
With a great big splash and a great big *bump!*

For now on people visit from all around
To examine this sad old boat.
You can see this little coat sticking out of the boat.

Emily Hawksworth (9)
Priory Junior School

If I Had Wings

If I had wings,
I would soar through the Milky Way,
Tasting bits as I go.

If I had wings,
I would touch a dragon
Smooth as a varnished gateleg table.

If I had wings,
I would listen to the roar of a lion
As deafening as crashing thunder.

If I had wings,
I would watch a dragon hover
Like a bird in the sky.

If I had wings,
I would sniff Martian tea,
As hot as a burning flame.

Robert Hannan (10)
Priory Junior School

If I Had Wings

If I had wings,
I would glide the deep blue sea
And talk with all kinds of exciting fish.

If I had wings,
I would soar up high into space
And see if the moon was really made of
delicious cheese.

If I had wings,
I would race the huge elephants
As they run away from a tiny, squealing, little rat.

If I had wings,
I would climb to the top of a beautiful rainbow
And stare at all the lovely colours.

Chanel Watson (9)
Priory Junior School

The Battle Of Bosworth

The armies lined up for battle,
One team, white roses,
And the other team red roses,
'Fire' shouts a man.

The battle's started,
Richard has 10,000 men,
The rage of people,
Fighting for victory.

Richard was looking for Henry,
To strike and be king,
People swinging swords to and fro,
Chopping everyone in the way.

Henry's archers were firing,
Blood and guts are dying,
Lord Stanley came to help,
With 5,000 men.

Richard charged down the hill,
And tried to strike Henry,
But missed,
Henry's soldiers surrounded Richard.

Richard had no choice,
Henry's men dragged Richard off his horse
And killed him,
Henry had victory.

A couple of months,
Henry's members found Richard's crown,
In a thorn bush,
And placed it on Henry's head.

Henry had victory!

Rhiannon Winwood (9)
Priory Junior School

If I Had Wings

If I had wings,
I would fly above a volcano,
and smell boiling breath of lava.

If I had wings,
I would feel Saturn
and touch its rocky rings.

If I had wings,
I would taste the sun
as hot as seething water.

If I had wings,
I would see the boiling lava
inside the Earth's crust.

If I had wings,
I would zoom to the moon
and hear the sound of space.

Louis Smith (10)
Priory Junior School

If I Had Wings

If I had wings
I would dance in the glistening crystals
that drop down from the moonlit sky.

If I had wings
I would float with the birds
in the cloud-clear blue.

If I had wings
I would soar up the mountains
to the snowcapped top.

If I had wings
I would float on the ocean
and swim the rolling waves.

Shauna Peace (10)
Priory Junior School

The Deserted Castle

In a dark graveyard,
Where a poltergeist lies,
Zombies wander,
Around the allotment.

In the castle,
Bats take over,
Come a cropper lights,
Around your face.

Slippery blood,
Blocks the path,
Spiders plunge from the wall,
Onto your face.

Homing arrows,
Follow you to the exit,
Ah, ah, ah, ah, ah, ah.

Dominic Thompson (9)
Priory Junior School

If I Had Wings

If I had wings
I would glide to France
and brush the top of the Eiffel Tower.

If I had wings
I would sniff
the scent of roses in a rose garden.

If I had wings
I would paint the world
pistachio-green.

Belinda Winfield (9)
Priory Junior School

The Bloody Battle

One summer day there was a battle
The battle was between Richard III and Henry Tudor,
Henry had 5,000 men but Richard had double.

When the battle had almost started,
Sir William came and evened it out,
So the odds were even and the battle commenced.

After a while the battle had finished,
With Richard off his horse,
But going to the dead,
The battle was a bloody sight.

Two weeks later the crown was found,
Found in a thorn bush,
Later on he was crowned Henry VII
Where he was crowned was Westminster Abbey.

Daniel Newman (10)
Priory Junior School

The Sunken Ship

The sunken ship I saw
When I dived down under shore
Then the ship came up
When I said the words, 'A ship?'

It came out a Viking ship
With skeletons rattling
In the wind
With thunder thrashing.

The ship stood there, dead
Then it gave a swish,
It went back to its country
Giving me bones in the post.

But what's best of all
It's gone.

Thomas Williamson (9)
Priory Junior School

If I Had Wings

If I had wings,
I would fly to the Earth's core,
And taste the orange glow.

If I had wings,
I would fly round the Earth,
And gaze at all its landmarks.

If I had wings,
I would fly the solar system,
And smell all its wonders.

If I had wings,
I would fly to the stars,
And feel its dazzling surface.

If I had wings,
I would fly to the rainforest,
And listen to all its wondrous animals.

Beverley Fletcher (10)
Priory Junior School

If I Had Wings

If I had wings,
I would float to Antarctica to touch the rapid sea
and race with the big furry Polar bears.

If I had wings,
I would slide slowly down the multicoloured rainbow
to find the pot of gold on the other side.

If I had wings,
I would see the tigers catch their prey
and see their natural habitats.

If I had wings,
I would fly to Australia to see
the bouncy kangaroos.

Kirstie Eldridge (9)
Priory Junior School

If I Had Wings

If I had wings,
I would soar along the sea
And talk to the fishes.

If I had wings,
I would go to Mars
And touch the cold, red sand.

If I had wings,
I would relax on a cloud
And have a drink with God.

If I had wings,
I would go deep into space,
And find amazing planets!

If I had wings,
I would do something
That no one's ever done.

Jordan Ulmer (9)
Priory Junior School

The Sunken Ship

Lady May,
Went down to the bay to find a sunken ship
'Oh gosh!' she cried,
And ran to the abandoned boat.
She looked around and found
A lot of dosh.
She took a golden hook
A few years on she realised it was good luck!

Katy Hinchliffe (10)
Priory Junior School

If I Had Wings

If I had wings,
I would touch the highest mountain,
and feel the cold, cold air.

If I had wings,
I would fly down, down,
and into the warmest and the bluest sea.

If I had wings,
I would fly up
and listen to the cry of the eagle.

If I had wings,
I would swoop down on villages
and see what life was like there.

If I had wings,
I would fly round castles of old,
and hear the ancient ghost's sword
clatter in the wind.

If I had wings,
I would watch plays in the great outdoors,
and see it from the bird's-eye view.

If I had wings,
I would fly over great seas,
and see all the wonderful birds fly down and catching fish.

If I had wings,
I would fly through Roman temples
before they fall to level ground.

Peter Kille (9)
Priory Junior School

Hawley's Darkness

I look up at the top of the tall castle,
to see a blue, small, shiny thing,
swooping into the castle.

All I can hear is the sea crashing,
against the castle wall.
I open the creaky door, I look around,
I really don't want to go in.

But something seems to push me in,
and locks me in.
I hear someone playing the piano,
from the top of the creaking stairs.

The door next to me swings open,
I see a chest,
I open the chest to see a mouldy skull,
I say to myself, 'This might come in useful.'

Now I go up the creaky stairs . . .

Amy Hamilton (9)
Priory Junior School

If I Had Wings

If I had wings,
I would stretch my wings up above Earth,
and listen to everybody talking.

If I had wings,
I would cast my eye over everybody.

If I had wings,
I would rest on the clouds
and smell perfume and sneeze.

If I had wings,
I would touch the sun and my fingers
would frizzle.

If I had wings,
I would nibble the moon and it would be
a fabulous toothpaste.

Matthew Chisem (10)
Priory Junior School

If I Had Wings

If I had wings,
I would touch the golden stars
as they sparkle over the world.

If I had wings,
I would fly to the countryside,
and smell all the beautiful flowers.

If I had wings,
I would taste the blazing sun,
burning in my mouth.

If I had wings,
I would listen to the drizzly rain
bash against the mountains.

If I had wings,
I would sneak into tomorrow
and plan my sunny day ahead.

If I had wings,
I would look into my future,
and see what I'll be.

If I had wings,
I would touch the fluffy clouds
as they float in the sky.

Hope Cooper (10)
Priory Junior School

If I Had Wings

If I had wings,
I would fly to Pluto
and taste a chunk
as cold as ice.

If I had wings,
I would fly to the edge
of the world and touch it.

If I had wings
I would fly high
up into the sky and
listen to the eagles.

If I had wings,
I would see
the beauty of the stars,
sun and moon.

If I had wings,
I would fly to the
top of a tall tree and
sniff the inside of an acorn.

Matthew Ascott (10)
Priory Junior School

If I Had Wings

If I had wings,
I would go to the moon and see if it tastes of soft,
yellow cheese.

If I had wings,
I would fly to the top of a tree and listen to the
howl of the wind.

If I had wings,
I would go to a lavender and smell the sweet fragrance
of it.

If I had wings,
I would go to Heaven and look for Almighty God.

If I had wings,
I would go to the forest in India and feel the
tiger's soft, stripy fur.

If I had wings,
I would dream of going in a dark, gloomy cave
and swinging with the bats.

If I had wings,
I would walk on the clear ocean waves.

If I had wings,
I would climb on the clouds and travel over the
blue and green Earth.

Robyn Staddon (9)
Priory Junior School

If I Had Wings

If I had wings,
I would go to the stars
to see what they feel like.

If I had wings,
I would taste the fresh
raindrops falling from
the sky.

If I had wings,
I would listen to the blackbirds
chirp.

If I had wings,
I would dream of smelling
all my favourite smells but
really be smelling the air.

If I had wings,
I would sit on the highest cloud
and watch the shooting stars go by.

Alyssa Ruston (9)
Priory Junior School

If I Had Wings

If I had wings,
I would go and feel the meteor's
rocky skin.

If I had wings
I would go and fly to the centre of
the Earth and listen to its tummy rumble.

If I had wings,
I'd fly up to the sun and smell its
red-hot chilli breath.

If I had wings,
I'd hover above the seas and taste its
salty waters.

If I had wings,
I would fly into space and ride the
tractor of stars and see what no one's
ever seen before.

Philip Mitchell (10)
Priory Junior School

The Three Divers

At the bottom of the cold and misty Atlantic
Ocean,
The haunted ship lies on the seabed,
The ship is rusty, mouldy and ruled by a ghostly captain
and his deadly crew.

The divers go down to find the treasure,
If they do it would give them great pleasure,
The divers fight with all their might, to find the
treasure.

They swim in the cabins and what do they find?
A shark and octopus too.
The three divers had to fight, the shark took a bite,
That left them with only two.

They swam on and saw the treasure,
As I said it was a pleasure,
They swam to shore, and got a cheer,
Then they went home and had a beer.

Nathan Donnachie (9)
Priory Junior School

If I Had Wings

If I had wings,
I would manipulate the sun's fiery individual
and feel the melting rock.

If I had wings,
I would flavour the fleecy clouds to see
how syrupy they are.

If I had wings,
I would hear the sound of the screaming
rockets through space.

If I had wings,
I would witness the furthest planets and
feel their icy shells

If I had wings,
I would scent the breath of a robust
roar of a dragon to see how much it
smells.

Jacob Hoster (9)
Priory Junior School

If I Had Wings

If I had wings,
I would glide up past the fluffy clouds
and watch all the people down below.

If I had wings,
I would savour a piece of the
Milky Way for deliciousness.

If I had wings,
I would soar up and up and
feel the fluffy clouds above.

If I had wings,
I would swoop around and hear the
sounds of a baby cry.

If I had wings,
I would smell the salty sea air
of the horizon.

Alice Dimmock (10)
Priory Junior School

If I Had Wings!

If I had wings,
I would go to Pluto,
and touch its cold surface.

If I had wings,
I would go to the high apple tree,
and taste its juicy apples.

If I had wings,
I would go to Mars,
and see all its mountains.

If I had wings,
I would fly high into the trees,
and smell all the blossom.

If I had wings,
I would go to the sun,
and hear the sun's volcano's erupt.

If I had wings,
I would fly to America,
and see tomorrow.

If I had wings,
I would go to Ghana,
and pick some of the cocoa beans
and taste them.

Jennifer Polhill (9)
Priory Junior School

The Battle Of Bosworth

Richard's troops on Ambien Hill,
No one's died in battle yet,
The score is still nil-nil.

Then someone shoots an arrow,
To start the battle off.
In a single second,
There's a soldier Henry's lost.

The battle's almost over now,
Thousands of people have died.
'I'm going to lose, I'm sure of it!'
Henry Tudor cried.

'Richard III is dead!'
That's the message that sends,
The Battle of Bosworth ield,
To a final end.

Grace Richards (10)
Priory Junior School

If I Had Wings

If I had wings
I would fly to the South Pole
and swim with the slippery penguins.

If I had wings
I would glide to a mountain
and look at the beautiful scenery.

If I had wings
I would skim the sea
looking at the scaly fish.

If I had wings
I would fly to the moon
and eat its cheese.

If I had wings
I would soar to the sun
and sunbathe.

Lewis Miller (10)
Priory Junior School

If I Had Wings

If I had wings I would feel
the wind go through my hair
as I fly with the birds.

If I had wings I would
touch the icy snow
at the North Pole.

If I had wings I would
listen to the sea lash
at the huge greasy rocks.

If I had wings I would
soar above the sea and
watch the fish leap out.

If I had wings I would
talk to people in
outer space.

Scott Griffiths (9)
Priory Junior School

If I Had Wings

If I had wings
I would taste the clouds
as sweet as candyfloss.

If I had wings
I would touch the end of Earth
and put my head into space.

If I had wings
I would listen to the seagulls
sounding like instruments.

If I had wings
I would gaze at the sun
seeing different colours.

If I had wings
I would dream to see polar bears
and climb on their backs.

Charlie Hoxley (9)
Priory Junior School

If I Had Wings

If I had wings
I would dream about floating
on white fluffy clouds.

If I had wings
I would slide down a rainbow
and feel the smoothness on my back.

If I had wings
I would watch the birds
as they swirl in and out of trees.

If I had wings
I would fly to the moon
and take a chunk of it home.

That's what I would do
if I had wings.

Matthew Nicholson (9)
Priory Junior School

If I Had Wings

If I had wings
I would chase the cheetah
on the lush green grass.

If I had wings
I would visit the kangaroo
and fly into its cosy brown pouch.

If I had wings
I would glide around the Earth
to see the beautiful colours.

If I had wings
I would see things no one has
ever seen before.

If I had wings
I would fly to the moon
and see if there were any cold-blooded aliens.

Andrew Laverty (10)
Priory Junior School

The Deserted Castle!

The castle was quiet
The castle was screaming
The door was open
Joseph was in.

There was a grunt
There was a stunt
Joseph kept walking
Joseph was listening.

Up the stairs
Down the quiet corridor
In the room
There was a grunt.

The castle was deserted
The castle was quiet
The castle was screaming
The door was closed?

Stuart Entwistle (10)
Priory Junior School

The Sunken Ship

On a spooky sunken ship,
the skeletons will drip,
with their bright red blood,
there's bound to be a flood,
on the sunken ship.

On a stormy night,
there's bound to be a fright,
for on the sunken ship,
the skeletons will drip
on the spooky sunken ship.

On the spooky sunken ship
the skeletons will drip
on a stormy night
there's bound to be a fright,
on the haunted, scary, spooky, sunken ship.

Seana Banks (9)
Priory Junior School

The Spooky Sunken Ship

The spooky sunken ship with skeletons aboard,
Their lives they couldn't afford,
They give their lives to save their ship
When all you hear is blood going drip
The spooky sunken ship.

The spooky sunken ship with treasure in there,
Treasure the price so very, very fair,
If you take that purse,
You get the curse of,
The spooky sunken ship.

The spooky sunken ship is the scariest of all,
Princes have fought with them all,
All of the princes die,
Because they're not the fighting kind of guy
The spooky sunken ship.

The spooky sunken ship is there today,
For you to go with your friends and play,
For you to play with your mate,
On any day or date,
The spooky sunken ship.

The spooky sunken ship has a sensation,
The spooky sunken ship, oh the fascination,
The spooky sunken ship is a true story,
Being the first to see it, oh such glory.

Rachael Bailey (9)
Priory Junior School

The Deserted Castle

Scary deserted castle
Worn away brick, go in, look around.
Dead bodies on the castle walls.

Scary deserted castle,
Armour, armour everywhere,
Passageway, can't get out.

Scary deserted castle,
Spiral stairway,
The gates are open.

Scary deserted castle,
Run, run quickly,
Bang, the gates are shut.

Scary deserted castle,
Up the stairway, along the wall
Escaped, escaped, escaped.

Jack Leenderts (10)
Priory Junior School

If I Had Wings

If I had wings
I'd fly up high with the birds in the sky,
and experience their life up there.

If I had wings
I'd follow the rainbow high and low
to find the gold.

If I had wings
You would find me under the sea
finding the most unusual animal
only I have seen.

If I had wings
I'd be up at Mount Everest
I'd fly up and touch the top
and fly back down.

If I had wings
I'd go to the desert
and meet the scary lion.
That's if I had wings.

Emma Christie (10)
Priory Junior School

If I Had Wings

If I had wings
I would climb a giraffe's back
and sit on its head.

If I had wings
I would fly on an eagle's back
and touch its head.

If I had wings
I would jump up and down
on the fluffy cloud.

If I had wings
I would touch every bright colour
of the rainbow.

If I had wings
I would take a chunk from Pluto.

Jade Hewitt (9)
Priory Junior School

Sea Life

Glittering and glimmering like a thousand stars,
Silent sea ripples in the light breeze,
All waves never-ending, on and on and on.

Golden sand like honey surrounding fish, crabs and eels,
All these things make the magical sea,
Rivers from everywhere leading into one big patch of water.

Sun shining down making heat on yourself,
Seaweed growing up between your toes.

Amy Hastings (9)
Queen Edith Community Primary School

The Spider

The spider is ebony-black.

He has a material to weave his special crystal,
And he moves like a bullet shot from a pistol.

He produces a velvety, delicate silk,
Which shines and glows like pearly milk.

He makes a most magnificent web,
In the shape of a dainty spider head.

His web sways slightly but swiftly in the April breeze,
But if he doesn't find shelter in winter, he will freeze.

Raindrops fall upon his treasure,
And give the spider excellent pleasure,
That the heavenly skies can transform his silk and dew,
Into a snowflake of pure frost.

He likes to swing from tree to tree,
He perseveres to repair his forever growing net of jewellery.

His favourite meal is a juicy fly,
Or any insect he can tie,
In his sticky home of royal silvers,
That he builds in trees or near rivers.

His dainty feet touch the ground,
Among the soil, but making no sound.

He likes the dank and dark hibernation,
Of the world's wonderful creation.

So to this day he still has a wonderful home,
Even though spiders don't roam,
The land, but for all eternity,
Spiders are brilliantly, superbly,
Skilled in all their excellent fame,
No other mini beast is the same.

Cordelia Chui (8)
Queen Edith Community Primary School

The Flood

Flood, help,
It's taking over like an invader
Under the door,
It's creeping up silently like a wild cat.
Halfway up the hall,
It's going to pounce soon.
On the first step,
It's a tiger.
On the third step,
It's a lion now, shaking its mane.
Fourth step,
Fifth step,
Coming up fast,
Sixth step,
Oh no! I've slipped,
I'm drowning,
I'm the prey.

Anna Collins (9)
Queen Edith Community Primary School

The Ocean

It wraps around me,
Like a big sea dog,
Lapping at my sides,
Grabbing at my body with ice-cold paws,
I rush to the surface,
Wrenching myself out of its grip,
Yet as I go it pulls me back,
Tormenting me,
Stealing my life,
I'm going,
Going,
Gone.

Ajit Niranjan (10)
Queen Edith Community Primary School

A Letter To Anne Frank

If I was there long ago
I would probably know
How much you lose
When I step into your shoes
Everything feels terrifying
All the toddlers and children crying
I feel terrified as well
When I hear that siren bell
Your diary made me think
When I make a link
To that war that you sat through
Boring and with nothing to do
Trying to not make much noise
When you drop all your toys
You must have thought it was silly
When you heard the news
About Hitler always despising Jews
Nothing different about you
I wish you were here
To have a long life
Not to go through all that war
It all must feel sore
I learned about you in Year 6
And then making a fix
On the scenery you are
Surrounded by
Not much to see
I bet you cried
Your eyes getting sorer and sorer
Bye for now, from a good friend, Laura.

Laura Di Paolo (11)
Queen Edith Community Primary School

A Letter To Anne Frank

It must have been hell for you
And all of it because you're a Jew
All cramped up in small places
The helpless looks on your faces.

I couldn't have managed all on my own
I would have hated to be alone
Being quiet from six to eight
Hardly any food on your plate.

Only one window to let air in
From dawn to dusk fear within
I couldn't have lived the life you had
I would have been so miserable and sad.

I couldn't live a life like you
Nothing to see, nothing to do
How could you have been so brave
I would have given anything to leave.

Your diary inspired every Jew
Everyone who reads it honours you
I couldn't have done what you did
I would have run away and hid.

How did you know what to do?
I wouldn't have been as brave as you
In your secret annexe you hid
Being silent with whatever you did.

Charlotte Bowden-Pickstock (10)
Queen Edith Community Primary School

Emotion

My anger is a burning rage, a disturbance hidden inside,
waiting to destroy.

My hatred is a vortex of darkness, a tiger waiting to pounce,
to attack the victim with all its strength.

My confidence is a sudden jolt, I attack with the speed of a cheetah.

My boredom is an endless pit of misery, nothing to attract
my attention,
an eternal sleep.

My happiness, a soaring eagle, reaching out for the sun,
attempting a daring feat.

My fear, I am being hunted, I must hide or I will soon end
my existence.

Karim Ahmed (10)
Queen Edith Community Primary School

The Storm

Trees falling, crack
Rain pouring like
Buckets of water.

Trees falling, crack
Wind whistling
Rain hammering.

Trees falling crack
Clouds black and moody
Clouds grey and angry.

Trees falling, crack
Lightning strikes
Houses on fire.

Jack Woodcock (10)
West Walton Community Primary School

With A Crash And A Bash!

Thunderstorm, rages, *crush!*
Windows broken with a *bash!*

People screaming feel like Hell,
Whoosh! Out comes the church's bell!

Whirling, swooshing hurricane
Everybody feeling pain.

Hurricane destroy and crash,
Thunderstorm begins to thrash!

Wind is blowing through your homes,
Dislocating all your bones!

Wind is lashing to your head,
It could be the one thing that you dread!

Storm is like a cheetah, stalking its prey
Homes being demolished, day by day by day!

Pressure on the whirling winds, crashing into trees,
Many animals scurry away, to get out of the breeze.

Ben Perrett (10)
West Walton Community Primary School

Windy Day

Daffodils prancing
Trees are dancing
On a windy day.

Sycamores piercing the air as they fly
Like helicopters falling from the sky.

Naked trees with no leaves
Swaying in the breeze.

Lee Plume (11)
West Walton Community Primary School

Night Of The Storms

Stormy night, stormy night
When dark and grey but calm
It starts little then more, until
Gale, gust, blitz, cyclone
Outbreaking, outbursting, whirlwind.

It stops for a while,
Before the downfall
Down, down, down it comes
Then comes the King.
Hurricane known as the terrifying clash.

Tornado as deadly as the lions
Battering, splintering, straining,
Wrenched, pressure, tearing,
Creating havoc,
Stormy night, stormy night.

Ben Gilding (10)
West Walton Community Primary School

The Sun

The sun is a giant torch scattering beams
of burnished gold.
It's a flaming yellow pearl.
The blinding brightness shines into our eyes
like a precious diamond.
The unclouded sun creates blazing, beaming,
beautiful, luminous beams.
The sun is a golden heart scattering beams
of happiness across the world.

Elliott Quinn (10)
West Walton Community Primary School

Storm

Drummers strike the sky
The storm passes by
Unpeopled streets
Currents of air blowing
Reservoirs filling
Candles glowing.

Waterlogged fields,
Gusty gale roars and moans
Rumbling draughts from out of this world,
Torrential downpours that numb your bones.

Defenceless animals dash to safety,
Seas charging like a furious stampede.
Then . . . just then with a flash,
Storm is still!

Daniel Cowling (11)
West Walton Community Primary School

Snow And Ice

Snow-topped mountains like ice cream,
Sheets of ice over streams,
Twirling, whirling round and round,
Blizzards deadly I have found,
Slabs of ice, like varnished wood,
Stay out of his way I know, I should.

Ice-capped mountains,
Snow-topped trees,
Shivering people, spine-chilling breeze,
Children trampling through the snow,
Great big snowballs they will throw,
Ice-capped mountains,
Snow-topped trees.

Edward Stagg (11)
West Walton Community Primary School

Power Cut

The storm swaggered into the night
like an evil creature looking for a fight.
It wrapped its arms around our home
Spoke with a low and frightful moan.

The lights went out and it all went black
I shouted out 'Mum, are we under attack?'
We had to have bread instead of toast,
We could not cook our Sunday roast.

I could not play my games or watch TV
As the storm came over me.
When oh when will the thunderstorm go
It's taken off the roof 'Oh no!'

We ate our tea by candlelight
And took our candles to bed that night.
Dad said things would be normal soon,
As I fell asleep by the light of the moon.

Kay Duggan (11)
West Walton Community Primary School

Thunder

Great black cloud cover over us,
Dismal sky cries upon us.
Why, why is the sky in a mood?
The roar is like a tiger for more food.
Bang, boom, barks away
It grows viciously.
The nursery turns to screams,
Then cries from baby's eyes.
People looking anxiously at the sky,
Then thunder goes by . . .

Jac Goult (11)
West Walton Community Primary School

Snowy Streets

Silver liquid drops dripping down my window,
While a blur of dots race down, down, down.
In our snowy streets.

Outside sheets of ice
Slipping, sliding round and round
People falling to the ground
In our snowy streets.

Snowmen being built up, torn down,
Dressed up, melting down
In our snowy streets.

Snowball shouting streets
Everybody having fun in the
Snowball throwing marathon
In our snowy streets.

Snowy streets such fun places to be
Hope the snowy days will come back
Next year.

Emily Bouch (10)
West Walton Community Primary School

The Blizzard

A bitter blizzard blows tonight,
It's coming to give me such a fright.
The penetrating storm pounds the roads,
I feel as though it's talking in codes.
A bitter blizzard blows tonight,
It's got me in its laser sight.

Jake Masham (11)
West Walton Community Primary School

Sun, Sun, What Is Sun?

Sun, sun, what is sun?
It's a burning fire of golden yellow,
As you stand in a burnished meadow.

Sun, sun, what is sun?
A sun dream when lying on a sizzling sunbed
'It's boiling out here, let's go in' I said.

Sun, sun, what is sun?
Above your head the sunlight gleams
I stand glaring up, as it sends down beams.

Sun, sun, what is sun?
The sun makes a clear fine day
As I play with my best friend Kay.

Now I know what
The sun is.

Sarah Gathercole (10)
West Walton Community Primary School

Dreadful Rain

Like an unwanted shower
Raindrops parade down
Filling glorious water towers.

Deluges down terrifying, amazing
Destroying freshly grown crops
Drowning innocent men.

Flooding beautiful meadows
Killing glorious flowers
Like lifeless souls.

Liam Gowler (11)
West Walton Community Primary School

A Storm

Lazering lightning striking on the trees,
Frightening all the animals into their homes.
When the storm has gone everything is ruined,
Dead trees and leaves laying on the ground.
Where the wind has swirled round and round,
A hurricane has been,
People's roofs are off,
Where a hurricane has been.

Robyn Vickers (10)
West Walton Community Primary School

Unbearable

The sun, an egg yolk frazzling in a frying pan
of a clear, cloudless sky.
Everyone feeling as sticky as glue
as the sun beams down.
Trees ablazing from the unbearable
rays of heat,
Red raw backs being revealed.
Sunburn, drought and trees on fire
are created by the sun.

Eilish Quinn (10)
West Walton Community Primary School

Blizzard

Blizzards are rough,
Blizzards are tough,
Blizzards a blinding storm
Blizzards are blazing,
Blizzards are racing,
Through the midnight sky.
They bash about from side to side
And no doubt they will leave you alone.

Karl Parry (11)
West Walton Community Primary School

Rain

Spitter-spatter the rain falls down
from the sky to the ground.
Splish, splash puddles appear
from the sky's grim lair.
Thunder, lightning, will come soon
with a great boom.

The rain makes the tide come in
it comes in slow and dim.
Pitter-patter on the windows
the rain falls and the wind blows.
Rain, rain everywhere
and not a space to spare.

James Woolford (11)
West Walton Community Primary School

The Snow

Snow drifts
As it comes smoothly on the ground
Like the wind as it comes gently in the sky.
Snow makes everyone feel cheerful.
Snow drifts
As it comes smoothly on the ground
Like the wind as it swifts gently into the sky.
Snow makes everyone feel cheerful.

Hannah Gathercole (10)
West Walton Community Primary School

Sunny Days

The sun is a glowing ball of fire,
Floating through the sky,
Sending blistering heat throughout the world.
Sun, sun, blazing out,
Using its blinding brightness.

The sun staring menacingly down on you and me
The sun is in an unclouded aqua-blue sky.
Always beaming,
Flowing contentedly through you and me
Until one day,
It's all gone.

Danielle Kirk (10)
West Walton Community Primary School

The Way Of Thunder

Rumble, crash, thunder, flash,
that is the way of the thunder.

Boom, bash, thunder, thrash,
that is the sound of thunder.

A big flash with a white lash
that is the look of thunder.

Rumble, crash, thunder, thrash
that is the way of the thunder.

Ashley Racey (11)
West Walton Community Primary School

Sunny Day

Sun burning fiery yellow,
burning on the golden meadow.

People putting on suncream,
from the sun's scorching beam.

Glistening down on everyone,
children having so much fun.

Laying on a chair,
men with their backs bare.

The sizzling sun dies away,
getting ready to come another day.

Abigail Barnes (11)
West Walton Community Primary School

Snow

Flakes swaying side to side
Snowballs flying in the sky
Crackle, crunch, snowman white
Icy roads for the night.
Snow sparkles like a light
Always glowing through the night.
Icy pond hard and cold
Thick and slippery and really bold.
Hats on heads and wrapped up warm
Fires burning in the rooms.

Lauren McLeod (10)
West Walton Community Primary School